HITCHHIKING THROUGH MANAGEMENT

MOORE'S 10 LAWS FOR SUCCESSFUL LEADERSHIP

PAUL MOORE

ISBN
Paperback 979-8-89632-495-9
Hardcase 979-8-89673-807-7

*To my friends, family and especially my wife Tanya.
The encouragement, input and support have
truly made this book possible. A person can only
be successful through a team effort.*

Contents

Introduction

So, you want to start the journey to being a good manager. As with any educational journey, the trip never ends and is full of ups and downs, twists, turns, and roadblocks, with occasional clear sailing.

I have been on that journey for over 40 years and in that time developed some good habits and learned lessons that I am going to share with you for your own journey. As the word "hitchhiking" in the title of this book implies, I would like to think that this transfer of knowledge will give you a lift to where you want to go in your management career. At the very least, it should alert you to some areas to watch out for. This book provides you with what I call "Moore's 10 Laws for Successful Leadership."

It wouldn't be a good story or, quite frankly, true-to-life if you didn't experience some failures or setbacks, and yes, I've had a few, too. But let's face it, they make the trip more interesting and at times you can even say fun, although it usually takes a while to see the positive side of seemingly bad experiences. If you're not prepared to weather some of those situations and have the opportunity to (one hopes) laugh about them along the way, then you are probably not cut out for management.

The germ of this book came from interactions and discussions I've had over the years with my teams. Many times, a bright ambitious worker would come into my office, seeking advice on how to become a manager. These moments typically made me smile and ask, "So, why do you want to be a manager?"

Great question, right? Since you probably picked up this book in the interest of pursuing that very same goal, or perhaps to improve your own management abilities, let's begin this leg of your journey to being a good manager together. At the end of the book, you should be able to understand how the question "Why do you want to be a manager?" is relevant to good management.

Before we begin, I think it's only fair to assess if this author has the background and experience to be credible. For that reason, it's important that we take a little time to know who Paul Moore is.

Paul Moore: An Overview

How you think, react to events, and respond to challenges results from the people who have influenced you and the experiences you have gone through. These are the building blocks of your life and who you really are. So, to understand who I became and how I evolved into a manager, it's appropriate to spend some time giving you a window into my life. This history should suggest how my thinking evolved and what led to the creation of Moore's 10 Laws for Successful Leadership.

My parents immigrated to Canada from England when I was two years old. When the boat and train rides were over, we settled in Southern Ontario. My dad was a mechanical engineer and my mom a pharmacologist, so it was mandatory that I would go to university. I excelled in math and was horrible in English. The irony is not lost on me that I am writing a book. My parents believed sports were very important and embraced their new country, so naturally I played hockey from age five. Unfortunately, my skating was less than stellar, so after two years of hockey, they enrolled me in figure skating to improve my skating skills. Figure skating was my first sports passion, although I will admit that, due to male stereotyping, initially I didn't jump into it with a lot of enthusiasm. As you can probably imagine, I was subject to my share of teasing and peer pressure—but my enjoyment and the success I experienced outweighed any pressure. Perhaps this experience was a big reason I am passionate about advising you to follow what feels right for you, but that's a whole other story we won't get into.

I focused on ice dancing and competed at the local levels until I was 15. It certainly taught me focus and how to deal with competitive pressure. At the peak of my training, I was skating six days a week and had little to no social life outside of the rink. Like most teenagers who want to experience other things in life, I chose not to continue down the competitive path but still wanted to complete my gold dances. That goal was given to me by a very wise coach, and it allowed me to turn professional and begin a career teaching general figure and power skating, with a specialization in ice dancing at the senior level.

Teaching was a great source of income for me as a teenager and through university. It also really helped me develop my communication and instructional skills. The most important of them, I believe, was using different approaches to help my students master a skill or move they didn't get right away. It became obvious that it was useful to have them understand an idea or concept we were trying to achieve and, through experimentation, find what worked for them. What made teaching skating particularly challenging was dealing with such a wide range of students: kids from age five through adults in their twenties. The levels of understanding differed significantly, and I had to learn to adapt my teaching style to each audience.

I received a degree in applied mathematics and computer science at McMaster University and later an MBA at the University of Alberta. I always enjoyed education and relished the challenges and in-class debates. Education has always been part of my life, and I have been constantly learning and upgrading my skills. My mother always said I was an annoying child due to my constantly asking, "Why?" Truly understanding something, whether it's emotional behaviour or the physical properties of objects, helps you gain perspective and potentially see another point of view. One thing I did learn: you never get to the root answer unless you ask why at least five times. You should look up the story of the little girl who asks her mother why she cut the end off the pot roast before cooking it; her mother answers that this is the way it has always been done. The payoff in this story about outdated traditions is a great reason to keep probing until you get the correct or real answer.

After my undergraduate graduation in 1983, the country was in a deep recession, with 16 percent mortgage rates, so getting work was a challenge. I decided to try the Canadian West, since my parents had moved to Alberta a few years earlier and really enjoyed the lifestyle. I accepted a position as a computer science lab assistant and part-time teacher of the computer programming language COBOL at Mount Royal College in Calgary.

A year later, I had my first information technology (IT) job at an oil sands plant in Fort McMurray. My first manager, Randy Olson, was a good manager. He always had time to listen to your ideas and encouraged and praised my work buddy Dave and me whenever we developed innovative solutions to help the business. After three years, I was given the opportunity to work in sales as a system engineer for the computer company Hewlett-Packard, or HP as most know it. HP developed some amazing management processes that I believe formed many of the core principles of my management style and which I have incorporated into Moore's 10 Laws. HP was also where I first managed a major project, the upgrade of the server technology for all the applications needed by the government of the Northwest Territories. This amazing opportunity required over 18 months of effort, with half of the time living in the arctic. The remote nature of the project forced me to be self-sufficient and sometimes required making quick and independent decisions.

Even with a successful career at HP, I was looking for new opportunities to develop my skills. So from HP I went to a leading computer network company, Ungermann-Bass, and ran its Canadian consulting services business. At that time, from the early 1990s onward, the importance of technology was growing exponentially for organizations, and I had the privilege of helping our client companies adapt to then new technologies like wireless (Wi-Fi), security firewalls, and voice over internet protocol, to name a few. The UB role enabled me to work with and manage people all over North America, and in the 1990s we were already pioneering virtual work groups and outsourcing.

During that time in my career I realized how geographic diversity and cultural differences definitely call for different management styles. With regard to outsourcing—at the time I was working with computer engineers in India to write code for Ungermann-Bass's network switching technology—I quickly realized how important clear communication was when managing overseas people. Management styles must be adjusted according to variations in geography and cultural norms, since what would be considered normal in one location was sometimes considered offensive in others. Even within North America, it is amazing how work styles and interactions differ.

With 12 years of experience in the vendor world at HP and Ungermann-Bass and a brief period of consulting on my own, I returned to the energy sector, working in the IT group for the next 20 years at Suncor Energy, with many managerial roles in the organisation.

The teams I managed over my career varied from 20 to 1,000 workers. Those teams, consisting of staff, college students in co-op programs, contractors, and cloud service providers, required many management styles. What was interesting is that even with those differences, I found that people are people and that certain core management techniques work in most situations—and those form the basis of the techniques compiled in this book.

Most influential to me, from a manager development perspective, were two experiences at Suncor. The first was the outsourcing of our IT services to a third-party organization, and the second was the multibillion-dollar merger of the two largest Canadian oil companies, Suncor and Petro-Canada, in 2009. Both events called for massive changes in the teams, roles, and responsibilities of one or both information services groups. During the merger, I was Suncor's acting CIO for the six-month transition, which included consolidating the delivery of information technology services from both staff and contractors. Single strategies needed to be executed, and redundant people and vendors let go. I found managing change is one of the most difficult responsibilities a manager has, particularly when it involves downsizing or assigning people to new roles.

After an amazing career with Suncor, I took early retirement in 2014 and pursued a more entrepreneurial life with my brother—a geophysicist and oil industry lifer—in a small oil exploration company he started up with two other engineers in southeast Saskatchewan. Although before my retirement I had also become the CEO of an investment company with 20 percent ownership of all the wells and production in my brother's company, once I retired from Suncor, I moved into a more active role in the operations side of my brother's company and since then have actively managed the monitoring of all production and have operated the plants when we need special projects completed or to relieve local operators when they go on vacation.

This position has required that I take a much more active role in the daily operations of producing oil, including monitoring and sampling the wells and oil treaters. The focus of management here is primarily on safety. Although I had spent much of my career working at oil companies and in plant environments, things are truly different when you must operate and perform maintenance on a plant with hazardous materials all around you. My maintenance work includes general repairs to piping, pumps, and control systems. Larger projects I have been involved with include winterizing the facilities, reconfiguring equipment and piping, and general optimization of the equipment.

When I retired from Suncor, I never expected my semi-retirement to be so...physical. That said, I keep in touch with technology through various startups and enjoy family time. My lighter workload has also allowed me to pursue my personal passions, the biggest of which is my love for flying. My childhood dream was to be a pilot. I think it would have made for a good career, but I am happy that I had the opportunity to obtain my pilot's license and have been flying recreationally for almost 20 years. In addition, piloting has fueled many areas of personal development that proved relevant to my managerial skills, stories of which I will share later in the book.

I'm standing in front of an oil rig in southeastern Saskatchewan in 2012. When you operate junior oil companies, you must be involved in all aspects of operations. Here we are drilling a horizontal well in the Bakken Formation, which underlies parts of Saskatchewan, Manitoba, North Dakota, and Montana. It's a high-risk, high-reward game with each well costing millions to complete. Decisions have to be made very quickly at any time of the day.

Spring 2014 in Victoria, British Columbia. Work-life balance has always been critical to my best performance. Most recently I became involved in triathlons, which allow me to vary my training between swimming, biking, and running. Here with my close friend Cloete Uys (left), then CIO of Pengrowth Energy, enjoying the competition at the 2014 Victoria Triathlon. The real satisfaction is reflecting on all the miles swum, biked, and run together for the big day.

An Overview of *Hitchhiking Through Management*

Why use the word *hitchhiking* in the book title?

I think hitchhiking is a very appropriate analogy for learning, in that hitchhiking and learning both allow for giving and receiving. Back when I was a teenager in rural Ontario, if you or your buddy needed to get somewhere and didn't have transportation, it was natural to just head out to the highway and stick out your thumb. You never knew who would pick you up, and usually you had some great conversations on a wide range of topics. Similarly, it was great to give a hand to someone who needed a lift, and they always had an interesting story or two to tell. Perhaps things were different in those days, given that today my wife looks at me with horror at the idea that I would even consider jumping into a stranger's car, let alone picking up a stranger in my own car.

I guess we believed most people were good and wanted to help. Plus, you never knew what you would learn. That really is the essence of this book: an interesting story or two from which you might learn something you never expected.

So, what are the origins of Moore's 10 Laws?

I believe good management can be based on 10 laws. I like the word *law*, since it implies a level of absoluteness and some degree of penalty if not followed. So, starting about 25 years ago, when I had discussions with people about their career or, say, while doing a performance review, I found myself repeating the same themes for areas they could work on. Most of the time, the advice concerned actions that could give them balance and success in their job.

I certainly didn't conceive of the running themes of this advice as "laws" until one such session, when one of my people quipped,

"You should make them your laws." So began the foundation of this book, the idea of Moore's 10 Laws for Successful Leadership. The label was a particularly fun way to talk about this advice due to my being one of a whole profession's worth of computer science nerds who were taught the very famous Moore's Law, named after Gordon Moore, one of the founders of Intel, who coined it in 1965. Wikipedia defines Moore's Law as the observation that the number of transistors in a dense integrated circuit (IC) doubles about every two years. Moore's law is an observation and projection of a historical trend. Rather than a law of physics, it is an empirical relationship linked to gains from experience in production.

People have since used Moore's Law to generalize that all computer technology (storage, CPU power, network speed) doubles every two years. Amazingly, even six decades later, that generalization continues to be the case, so it really is a good law. At least for now, of course!

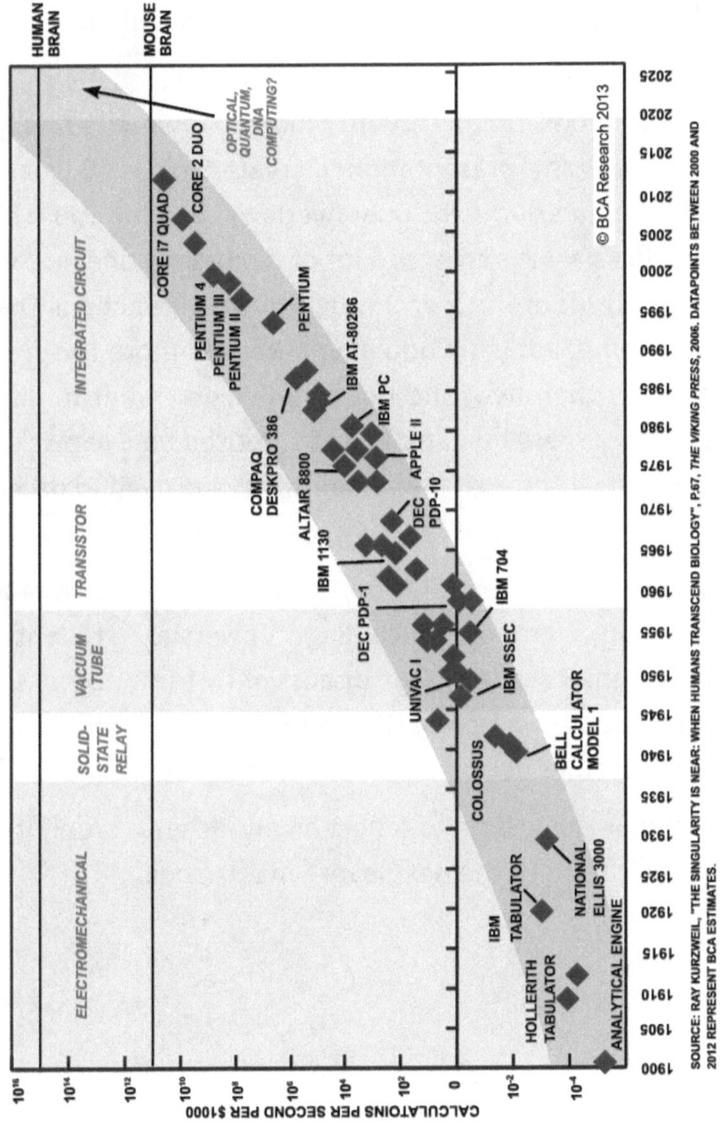

Figure 1. This graph demonstrates (Gordon) Moore's Law as it relates to computer processor technology and the number of instructions per second that each type of technology can complete. Moore's Law of doubled processing power every two years has held true since the early 1900s.

Unfortunately, Gordon Moore is no relation to me, but it has been amusing to apply Moore's Law in discussion and having some people in an audience think I'm some sort of famous genius.

Sorry, I'm just a person with a reasonable amount of common sense.

Workplace discussions of (my own) Moore's Laws eventually turned into a PowerPoint presentation I created over 20 years ago. The presentation started with only five laws, but the topic of management practices always creates a lot of discussion, and, in the spirit of (the original) Moore's Law, through those interactions the laws expanded to ten. (Sadly, my doubling pace was more like five to seven years rather than two, and I definitely didn't want to add any more. The limits of mere humans!) I was surprised how copies of the presentation made it through the organization and even to other companies.

I have spoken on the subject of Moore's 10 Laws for Successful Leadership to many groups, including university students, professionals, and senior leaders. Our discussions of (my) Moore's Laws have always created great back-and-forth interaction, and I always enjoy hearing other people's perspectives and suggestions.

So now, given that I have time to reflect on my life and career, it's time to take Moore's Laws to the next level—in this book.

Why Have These Laws?

As I mentioned in the introduction to this book, I started my career after graduating as an instructional assistant at Mount Royal College in Calgary. One of my responsibilities was to teach computer programming classes, which included helping students with the programming assignments.

The interesting thing about computer programs is that there are always many solutions or ways to accomplish the same function. This was an interesting challenge for me as an instructor, since you had to adapt your mind to the logic the student was using for the problem or assignment. Most would accomplish the goal and their outputs would be correct, but they all followed very different paths. Each student's solution had advantages and drawbacks, but the key was that if they remained consistent in their logic, their solution worked.

This is a life lesson I'm sure you have heard is relevant in many scenarios: being consistent with whatever logic you use will generate positive results. Probably the easiest, most relatable example of applying consistency is that of parenting. Everyone agrees that each child is unique, and it would be nice if they came with a manual. But if you are consistent with your rules and reactions, most children will respond well and won't try to push the boundaries (well, not too much).

I do emphasize *most* children, since it is an amazing phenomenon with humans that you can say or do the same thing with two people and get very different results. My mother used to tell people how challenging it was to parent three boys. As an example, she would tell a story of when we three had done something really bad (yes, we were always getting into some form of mischief) and were sent to our rooms to reflect on our behaviour.

After giving us some appropriate period of time to reflect on our evil ways, she would prepare to speak to each of us independently.

Since I was the oldest, Mom usually would come into my room first, and apparently I would say something like "Mommy, I am so sorry, I won't do that again."

Feeling very satisfied with the parenting she had done, she proceeded to the middle brother who, when she entered his room, would shoot her his evilest look and say, "I hate you and will never forgive you."

Finally, a little confused at the completely different reactions of her first two boys, Mom would enter the bedroom of our youngest brother. There he would be quietly playing on his bed and would look up and say, "What did I do?"

So goes the dilemma of dealing with individuals. You may have to be careful with your coaching and managing techniques, since each can evoke very different reactions.

I believe management is no different and having a consistent, repeatable style will enable you to succeed. That said, you may have to use a different style for different people. Unfortunately, the only way to know what approach to take will be through trial and error. Once you build up your understanding of the way each person interacts or responds, repeat the relevant method with that individual.

These laws were my foundation for being consistent in my approach and decision-making. I believe they have been of great assistance in most of my achievements throughout my career and life.

It is very important that I qualify the laws I will discuss in this book with the phrase "from my perspective." Rather than using this phrase ad nauseam throughout, I offer the caveat that readers should assume that all of my opinions and findings are from my perspective. I freely admit that I have views or perspectives in life that result from my experiences and teachings, and they can be very different from yours.

The story that best describes perspective and the importance of complete text or information to me is the famous one about the blind men and the elephant. Its earliest versions are found in Buddhist, Hindu, and Jain texts.

If you are not already familiar with it, here is the story.

A group of blind men heard that a strange animal, called an elephant, had been brought to town, but none of them knew its shape and form. Out of curiosity, they said, "We must inspect and know it by touch, of which we are capable." So, they sought it out, and when they found it they groped about it. The first person, whose hand landed on the trunk, said, "This being is like a thick snake." For another one whose hand reached its ear, it seemed like a kind of fan. Another man, whose hand landed upon its leg, said, "The elephant is a pillar, like a tree trunk." The blind man who placed his hand upon its side said, "The elephant is a wall." Another who felt its tail described it as a rope. And the last felt its tusk, stating that the elephant was hard, smooth, and like a spear. All of the men were, of course, only partly right, because each had only a partial perspective.

Source: Wikimedia

Since most things in your life are usually like an elephant, I have always sought to understand different perspectives and opinions, which help us grow and gain that complete view of something. Ideally if you had perfect information, you would always make the perfect decision, but sadly life is imperfect and sometimes seeking all or as much information as possible is not cost effective or viable in a situation with time constraints. Good management is about balancing time and effort and, by using the information available, making the best decision at that moment. A critical attribute for you will be a willingness to see other perspectives and adjust your view accordingly.

And now we are ready to address my own perspective, encapsulated in Moore's 10 Laws for Successful Leadership.

Moore's First Law

If It's Not Written,

It's Not Real

If you remember only one rule from this book, this is it. Have you ever been caught between two parties arguing over something, and you are trying to help resolve the dispute? Of course you have. In fact, resolving disputes seems to be the primary role of management these days.

Let me give you an example of how most of these conversations have gone for me as a manager. We shall call this the recipe for Moore's First Law:

Step 1.	An employee walks into my office with fire in their eyes and smoke coming from their ears (I'm sure you relate to this scenario).

Step 2.	A passionate story erupts of how some third party is completely incompetent or has royally screwed them over.

Step 3.	At the triumphant conclusion to the story, where throwing the other party in the brig seems totally justified, it seems logical to me to ask a simple question, Why has this happened?

Step 4.	This is usually the long part. Now we go into a detailed discussion of the project or assignment that has flown off the rails. We delve into how it has gone completely in the wrong direction, or the scope has exploded, or why, all of a sudden, the customer has seemingly changed their mind. You can likely recount your own personal experience with meetings like this. I have observed that most of the time throughout the story, the complaining employee has emphasized to me that the situation was plainly obvious and that everyone had always understood and agreed to what was happening.

Step 5.   Now is the time I like to stop the conversation and ask my favorite question: "Could I please see the documentation for and correspondence about the work?" The typical response has been: "Ah well, we had a conversation (sometimes even a meeting), and I told them, and they understood."

Really, that's your defence?

So much in management is about ensuring clear understanding. How is it possible to achieve clear understanding, or even make a judgement on something, when all you have is a story someone told and the other party heard? The only thing organizations can fall back on is the written word, so naturally Moore's First Law is:

IF IT IS NOT WRITTEN, IT IS NOT REAL.

It's not perfect by any stretch of the imagination, and the level of detail will always vary with the complexity of the situation, but Moore's First Law is the best tool for giving guidance and helping work stay on track. I'm not suggesting that everything must be a contract, and we'd need to get lawyers and/or the supply chain involved. The right level must be used for the right purpose.

Having things written is critical, as I have discovered. Here are just a few examples that I hope will reinforce the reasons underlying this law and make it more relatable.

Status Reports and Dancing Ants

I don't think you can avoid dealing with status reports, and from a team perspective they are time-tested and probably the most efficient way to track ongoing activities within operations, projects, initiatives, and general communications. Almost all management, project, and sales tools have status reports built in. Over time status reports have been made more efficient to enter data into and update, but I believe that creating them is a particularly hated job task, and people usually do not do them well. But if properly used to document actions, next steps, and resolutions they can be a powerful source of learnings, resolutions for new problems, and guidance for new projects.

They also have an interesting secondary effect of ensuring that people are held accountable for their statements and commitments. After all, the status report makes everything visible in black and white. A very good manager of mine at Suncor, Joe, was amazingly meticulous when creating and maintaining status notes. He used a very interesting style to draw attention to items, one worth sharing with you. Early in my Suncor career, when the IT departments were decentralized across the country, Joe chaired our monthly IT council meeting. We always started the meeting by reviewing the current status report that contained a running list of activities and tasks for the IT organization to complete. Every action had a status, a date for completion or update, and the name of the member (the "owner") to whom it was assigned.

When we were on an item, either its owner reviewed any updates by citing the notes they had entered (which wasn't very often!) or it was reviewed live and verbally. Further actions were then documented immediately. Joe was always the scribe. If the update was completely unchanged since the last meeting or the timeline was slipping, Joe would visually represent the status. Since we were using

PowerPoint, he had some interesting ways to do that. With the first unsatisfactory update or missed date, the item was converted from black to red type. As you can imagine, this change made those items obvious in a report and helped members focus on the escalation and its requirements. If a status item was missed a second time, the item was now underlined in red. If that wasn't enough attention, we progressed to, as it were, a third level of shame. Ever resourceful, Joe found a fascinating feature in PowerPoint that highlighted the text and put a set of flashing lights around the item. Once, when we first spotted an item in red underlined type surrounded by flashing lights, one of our directors described the highlights as "dancing ants."

We developed a great team over the years, and the escalation process was taken in good spirits. Certainly anyone whose item received the dancing ants treatment was teased quite heavily. But the point was well understood, and Joe never needed to create an even more severe degree of highlighting in the status report.

Seeing something on a screen has a very powerful effect, particularly when it is flashing. But if nothing had been written down, we wouldn't have had a visual representation of what had been completed and what still needed to be done—and we wouldn't have remembered what cans were getting kicked down the road indefinitely.

Change Management

Anyone with operational role experience understands the importance of controlling an operating environment. If you want to change something, it is critical that change is documented at a minimum. Change management, as we look at it through the lens of management in this book, is the structured process where an organization controls any changes introduced to a system or the organization itself.

When I was just out of university in my first job as an IT operator (in the days when we actually had to mount magnetic tapes for the mainframe to read), I was amazed at how the system administrator for the minicomputers would come to the computer room and reset the computer or load some new software without any heads-up or communications. Users were very accustomed to systems going down and would simply go out for coffee and wait for them to come back online. Given that we lived in a plant with an operations environment, many of our users were engineers. I will let you in on a secret: plants don't like interruptions, so this behaviour was not destined to last for very long since computer systems were becoming more and more critical to running operations. So, in the early 1980s operations engineers helped us (as if we had a choice!) improve the IT service for the organization by bringing change management to the department.

In the late 1990s at Suncor, I was the manager responsible for bringing in the change management process and systems to enable a structured governance and reporting of all changes in the IT environment. In an operating environment like a plant, the personnel that support it must submit a request to alter the operating conditions. The alteration might be to replace equipment or to do routine maintenance like changing the oil in an engine. In any case, the task must be submitted to the change management process to screen it for risk and impact as well as for what would to do if the change negatively affected plant operations. When approved, the change can be scheduled and clear communications sent to all affected parties. At Suncor it became clear to me that as computer systems became more of a necessity in the workplace, our systems analysts would have to govern the systems supported by those computers, just as they would in any plant environment. So we started treating the information technology environment as a plant, and thus all modifications to that plant had to be governed by change management.

Properly implementing change management in IT organizations has been a challenge over the last 40 years. But the very structured documentation and approval process has, in my career, provided many benefits:

- Written understanding of what is being changed allows others in the organization to flag any overlaps or conflicts with the proposed change.

- Documented steps allow efficient and reliable backout procedures.

- Interruptions of service can now be clearly communicated and articulated to the user community, and they would have input on schedule to minimize work disruption.

- Problem resolution within the IT environment can be increased dramatically, since, in change management, the first step of problem analysis is now, "What has changed?" All changes (of which there were usually at least 50 in any week at our company) can quickly be reviewed and analysed to see if they contributed to the problem.

Along with these benefits, however, it is clear that overzealous documenting and approving of changes can result in the negative effect of undue administration, overhead costs, and a lack of timely action for required changes.

A great example of that overzealousness occurred years later at Suncor once change management had become embedded in the organization. I had moved into a corporate role but enjoyed keeping up with what was happening in the field where I had spent the early part of my career. On one such trip, I asked how things were going and was surprised to hear about the difficulty the users at the oil sands plant were having getting new computers installed or even moved. Some requests were taking over two weeks! Back in the day, we IT technicians used to handle this kind of request within a day. After hearing the complaint, I wandered over to the network group to chat with some of the technicians about the delays. I couldn't believe my ears when some very young newbie explained how they had changed management up in the plant and all the forms and approvals (which occurred only once a week) were required before they could connect a computer to the network. I basically lost it and immediately barked at this tech, "Listen, buddy (the cue by which everyone knew I was really annoyed), I created change management up here before you were out of school, and I can guarantee you it was never meant to apply to a task that takes less than a minute to do." Needless to say, we modified the process with the IT management team at the plant.

Defining the balance and level of change management requires thorough benefit and cost analysis. But it is still a great example of how writing something down improves the work environment.

Decision Logs

Having a well-defined decision log is essential for organizations to avoid misunderstandings about what decisions have been made and to avoid revisiting the same item many times. I will speak more about decisions in Moore's Seventh Law.

Matrices (Example: Risk Management) and Manuals

Matrices and manuals are other good examples of making things real by writing them down. A matrix by its nature is complicated to explain without a visual representation. Typically, matrices are two-dimensional, so they show a specific answer or action from two sources of inputs. Some matrices can have hundreds of inputs and therefore possibly thousands of permutations that are very easily identified when presented in a written tabular form. If you expand a matrix to a third dimension, then tracking the information for all three inputs is almost impossible without its being written or illustrated.

Manuals are usually more of a linear step-by-step document where the sequence is critical. It is a serious issue if an operator of a plant does not have the written procedure in front of them when they start up or shut down equipment. You may have done something hundreds of times, but what if a procedure has changed since the last time you did it?

This exact situation happened to me when I was flying with an approach chart to an airport that had been updated literally the day before my flight. I made the mistake of not updating my manuals before takeoff. It is not only embarrassing but very dangerous—with the possibility of mid-air collisions—if you assume you know the approach procedure and it has changed.

My dad spent many years at the Bruce Nuclear Generating Station in Ontario. One of his roles was as a shift supervisor operating the plant. As an engineer in his past roles, he had been one of the people responsible for updating operating procedures. I learned from him that any operator who was caught without the operations manual in front of them open to the correct page was immediately dismissed. Nuclear power plants do not react well if the correct steps are not followed, and safety was the highest priority (as it should be) in that environment.

Contracts

Contracts are probably the most interesting written documents in our workplace. I'm sure they are the most reviewed and argued-over items when they are being created you will ever experience. Interestingly, though, they are the most unreferenced paperwork during their lifetime. I always say that when a deal or relationship is going well, no one ever discusses the contract. Only when you have a disagreement or conflict does this document ever get used.

For that reason, if you are involved in signing contracts, take that extra time and be sure you understand all the items and their implications. Lawyers ensure that they minimize their clients' risks and exposure. Diligence is required to ensure that all loopholes are closed.

A Pilot's Checklist

On a personal example of needing things to be written, I want to tell you a story about flying. As I've mentioned earlier, one of my lifelong dreams was to be a pilot, and in my forties I had the opportunity to become one and earned my license. Over the years I enhanced my pilot's license with night, mountain, and finally instrument ratings. Achieving the last rating is very challenging, since it is basically flying only by your instruments, allowing you to fly safely in conditions of zero visibility. I found flying exhilarating, and it appealed to my sense of precision and order in executing a task.

The one element of flying that is drilled into you is procedures and checklists. No pilot steps into the pilot's seat until they have performed a complete external inspection following the manufacturer's checklist. You cannot begin your flight until you are satisfied that your plane is in working order and you have the correct amount of fuel on board. In small planes you cannot trust your gauges. You have to physically dip into your tanks with a measuring stick to get a visual confirmation of how much gas you have. Let's face it, who wants to run out of gas at 10,000 feet above the ground?

Now you are ready to start your airplane, taxi to the runway, and take off. Every aspect of operating that aircraft is documented in your pilot's checklist. No matter how many times you have flown, you always have your checklist out and step through the active procedure (takeoff, landing, etc.), all the while verifying every item or action. This is critical, since missing even a single step can be disastrous. It is also something that can save your life.

As an example, I was flying the plane my brother and I owned over Northern Ontario, following the north shore of Lake Superior, when I had a catastrophic engine failure. Thanks to literally hundreds of hours of training and the trusty pilot's checklist, which includes procedures for engine failure, I quickly began the processes of assessment and action items.

Following procedures is critical, since the first step is to set the plane into a steady glide configuration so you don't stall out of the air, then attempt to fix the engine problem. When the engine restart didn't work, the next step was to call ATC—air traffic control—to declare an emergency. Our conversation went something like this:

Pilot: Mayday, mayday, mayday. ATC, this is Gulf Gulf Kilo Quebec [the plane's call letters, GGKQ] with an engine failure. Flight level 13,000.

ATC: Gulf Gulf Kilo Quebec, acknowledge your situation. Marathon Airport 42NM on bearing 070, can you make it?

Well, that was an interesting question. A quick calculation of my glide ratio showed the distance I could cover with no engine was 25 nautical miles. The engine was still running with about 20 percent power and a lot of smoke so my answer to ATC was: "I will try."

What followed was probably the longest 15 minutes of my life. What transpired during that period was a juggling of me coaxing the airplane to stay in the sky and managing the multiple conversations I was having with ATC. Actually, I was fortunate that an Armed Forces helicopter was in the area and was coordinating its location with me in case I needed to land in the bush. You must understand that this area of Northern Canada basically is all rocks and trees and small lakes. What's more, it was February, so everything was snow-covered and, to say the least, very inhospitable.

As it happened, I managed to coax that extra 17 nautical miles out of my sick plane and was very pleased to see that runway in front of me. Five minutes later, I was gliding my plane onto the runway for a pretty good downwind (not ideal, but I had calculated that I didn't have the altitude to come around for a proper into-the-wind-approach) dead-stick landing, if I do say so myself.

My point is to illustrate the power of my procedures and written checklists that, with training, helped me execute the steps to land the plane safely. In a stressful situation, it's best not to rely on your memory!

The Bottom Line

I heard a great saying in a class once that, given the same information, reasonable people come up with the same result or answer. Applying this philosophy, written information is an excellent way to ensure everyone is working from the same information and therefore should come up with the same conclusion. Writing is not perfect, since human nature means that we also tend to use our additional, unshared knowledge about a given subject, including past experiences or familiarity with the personalities of people involved. For example, you may have worked with another leader in a department who believes their team is the best at dealing with activities in their group. Basically, they hate outsiders. This information is valuable in assessing the likelihood of cooperation with this team and how to structure delivery of any services. Potentially the decision may have to be discussed at a more senior level with individuals who are open to new suggestions and methodologies.

In summary, make sure the language is clear. The growth of social media comes with an explosion of tools to communicate with. Many new short forms of language have emerged, leading to frequently misunderstood messages, particularly concerning intent. Were you trying to relay anger, humor, sadness? Sarcasm (one of my favourite tools) is very difficult to convey in writing and quite frankly should probably be avoided at all costs. Taking a few minutes to reread what you have written with a consideration of how the receiver might interpret it often saves you from losing time on the back end recovering from misunderstandings.

Even if you don't want to write down a conversation or meeting, record it. You can then simply tag the information and store it in a data repository. Do not underestimate the importance of tagging, since finding information in today's world can be a challenge.

Moore's Second Law

They Lie

This law is definitely my favorite and usually gets the greatest reaction from people when you simply say, "They lie." To be fair, "lying" is probably too harsh a word for what the law tries to convey, but people do remember it. The bottom line or the intent behind Moore's Second Law is that most people don't give accurate or complete information.

Types of "Lies"

Some reasons I've found over the years that people have "lied" to me are:

- ***They underestimated the time and effort a task or action was going to take.*** This underestimation is the most common reason in the work environment. Primarily, this is due to the lack of having all the information required to make a highly reliable estimate, which realistically is virtually impossible to achieve. You will always have situations where various requirements or gathering information take longer than anticipated, or when you try to build something and realize you don't have the right tools, or when high-priority and/or "break-in" work takes precedence.

- ***They didn't understand the requirements or deliverables.*** It is actually very hard for people to articulate their wants or needs. As an example, you can get a request to build something, and you make assumptions of what they want based on the discussion or description they gave you. On the other person's side, usually they too have made assumptions, such as that you knew what they meant, even if they did not explicitly state or communicate it.

  To illustrate this point, let's use a homebuilder whose customer requests that they build a house. As you can imagine, this request requires a lot of interpretation: How big? How many floors? How many bedrooms, bathrooms? Carpet or wood flooring? Colors? I realize that this is a simplistic example and only scratching the surface of the decisions required when building a home, but it's pretty clear to see that details matter to both parties with such a large and personal investment. There's a need to be as clear as possible, with many opportunities for misunderstanding.

One great way of establishing mutual understanding among multiple parties is to use examples and models. I truly believe in the adage "a picture is worth a thousand words." It's also why homebuilders create model homes. The hundreds of details that need to be agreed upon would take too long to discuss, and blueprints make things very hard to visualize.

- **They embellished or exaggerated.** Sometimes you have someone who wants to please or seeks recognition. I'm not suggesting that these are bad traits. In fact, an article that appeared in the *Harvard Business Review* in 2021, "A Little Recognition Can Provide a Big Morale Boost" by Shibeal O'Flaherty, Michael T. Sanders, and Ashley Whillans, concluded that praise and recognition are better motivators and last longer than monetary rewards.

  But constantly seeking recognition can make people overzealous and may lead them to embellish a situation or exaggerate it. As a manager you must question and double-check people's statements for accuracy and ensure they are providing complete disclosure. Sometimes it's really okay, in a friendly way, to ask if they might not be exaggerating a little bit.

- **They told you what you wanted to hear.** I love the saying, "My mind is made up, don't confuse me with the facts." A great illustration of this saying happened to me when I was the head of the IT group at a large plant. It was budget time and, as always, we were being instructed to tighten our belts. In those days we used computers on-site as our method of distributing the cost of IT services, and forecasting the growth of those workstations was critical in determining the IT requirements and costs. My team had done a great job of pulling all the workstation requirements in the last three years and we were entering into a growth phase of the business, expanding the size of our location. We had agreed the growth curve of the workstations would stay similar and we would add approximately 10 percent, or 800 computers. But in the management review of our budget, this increase was deemed unacceptable, and I was told very firmly that all organizations had been polled and they would not need any new computers.

Perhaps I was young and not as politically astute as I should have been, but my response was, "They are lying." Needless to say, that didn't go over too well and I was told to set the budget for zero growth. Nobody wanted to admit they were going to need the computers, and they did not appreciate my telling them something to the contrary. Well, you can guess, at the end of the year we had increased the number of computers by slightly over 800 machines, and we had blown our budget. As an add-on to Moore's Second Law, I strongly suggest that, in situations like the one I just described, it is unwise to follow up with the phrase "I told you so." It's probably worse than telling leadership they lie and no, I wasn't stupid enough to put both feet in my mouth, LOL.

- ***They said whatever it took to close the deal.*** I want to be on the record to tell you that some of my best friends are sales reps. I have spent several years in sales roles and have a deep respect for that role and how difficult it can be. The rejection factor alone is very difficult, and successful salespeople have tremendous resilience. That being said, in my roles of support analyst and project manager, I have heard some amazing stories from my sales reps about how phenomenal a certain product or solution was, and that it would do exactly what the customer asked for. I usually would follow up the meeting or presentation with the salesperson and ask if they were insane. One of my favourite reps I worked with over the years would just smile at me and say, "I have every faith in you to make it happen." Generally, I would rise to the task and achieve the impossible about 50 percent of the time, but that still left a lot of people unhappy with the result.

How to Avoid Being Tripped Up by "Lies"

As managers, what actions can we take to mitigate the risk of "lies"?

1. Spend time really understanding the requirements. Get agreement on the end product or service you are trying to achieve. In my experience, the greatest success came from rapid prototyping and engaging with the user. A great example of this I saw in the movie *The Founder* (2016), a biographical drama about the founding of McDonalds. No, the founder was not businessman Ray Kroc—the original founders were the McDonald brothers, who worked and reworked the process of making burgers and fries in the interest of efficiency. It just didn't happen, until they acted out various kitchen activities, marking their movements with tape on the floor and making important discoveries in the process. Doing so beforehand was far more cost-effective than building the kitchen and having to modify it later.

   A secondary benefit of engaging your user or customer in the requirements phase is their complete buy-in. After all, they have now helped create the project. We must expect that most people don't really know what they want and more than once I have heard people say, "I will know it when I see it." Prototyping and engagement will help you achieve alignment in requirements and deliverables. This alignment will then remove many of the situations where you feel that people have "lied" to you.

2. You will rarely work on something completely new that has never been done before. At best, you may have a situation where the blocks of work have never been arranged in this manner, but each element has been done before. For this reason, when you discuss actions, scope, and timing of work, it's a great use of time to ensure that the team has pulled historic information including

the other projects' or activities' results and, if you are lucky, the findings. Doing so will greatly increase the likelihood of your accurate delivery of the project within the required scope on time and on budget.

3. Don't forget to factor in rework, testing, change management, documentation, and training. Every one of these elements of work will get a lot of pushback from your team, your customer, and your own company management. Most view these activities as overhead, but I cannot emphasise how critical each is to successfully delivering your work and ensuring *you* are not perceived as lying.

4. Always build in a buffer for whatever you are committing to. It should always be well understood that you are doing this, since many people do put in buffers and don't reveal it. I have used the term "sandbagging," which accurately represents this practice of not revealing the existence of and the rationale for buffers. For some strange reason (I have never investigated the detailed analytics of this phenomenon), the rule of doubling has worked very well in my career. As an example, if a team told me we would have something operational in a month, generally it was available and live in two months. Something for you to consider in your area.

Moore's Third Law

It's Just a Game, Don't Take It Personally

created this law to try to help people who seem to take things too seriously and very personally, particularly at work. Don't get me wrong, I suffered from being a workaholic and became very intense when I was under pressure or had a time crunch on a project or sales proposal. Many times I have been up the whole night completing something, which definitely takes the fun out of life.

My favourite situation (but only in retrospect) where I took something too seriously occurred when I was working for a networking company in an intense sales situation. We had to make a big presentation and demo for a Canadian government IT department that ran on the IBM operating system. The software for the demo needed to be installed, but only one computer in our office ran the IBM operating system. Yes, can you believe there was a time we didn't use Microsoft Windows? Anyway, the product we were demoing was the company's network management tool, and we could not get the product to run on this particular workstation. I must have reloaded and configured that system a dozen times that night. Finally, at 6:00 a.m., our company lab gave us some configuration changes to try. There was only enough time to load the changes and bundle everything up so we could head to the customer.

Our sales team waited with bated breath, trying to look calm in front of the customer while I hit the power button and anxiously waited for the machine to boot. In those days with this software, the loading process took around five minutes, and those five minutes were truly the longest wait in my life and quite frankly were way more stressful than they should have been. Thankfully the story ends well: the product worked, and we proceeded successfully with the demo.

Another common situation that used to get to me was competitive bidding, when the organization we were submitting a proposal to simply used us to leverage a better deal with another vendor. Doing so isn't wrong and is realistically a good business decision. It just hurts when you feel you have been busting your butt and burning the midnight oil on something you really had no chance of winning.

Sometimes I think we did things like that for the rush and the feeling of winning a deal or being the saviour. This does have a dark side, however, when you don't win it and fail. The low on the other side of losing is just as intense if not more. Without the right frame of mind, one can develop very serious stress and depression, which can be very hard on your health, not to mention on your ability to think clearly and make sound decisions going forward.

Through my career, I managed hundreds of people directly and tried to be a good manager, learning from people who managed me and having an open style. One area I take personally is being able to read people and help them before something becomes serious. Sadly, I had two people who required an absence due to stress. What made these situations hard for me was that I didn't see the signs; some people can be very introverted, and burnout often does not manifest itself until it is serious. You never want to have people become physically ill for a job.

So, why not think of your work like a game? The workplace should be a healthy environment with good sportsmanship, as we learned and (it is hoped) developed throughout our childhood. A game has rules and standards of conduct, a beginning and, most important, an end. Normally we play a game because it's fun, it tests our abilities, and we feel good when we do well. I don't know about you, but these principles sound like they can be directly applied to the work environment in a positive way.

So, if we use the game analogy for work, we need some principles to govern it. As with any game, you should:

- Give it your best.

  - *When you are at work, it is important to give it 100 percent. Management always appreciates effort and should always recognize and reward it. The reward can be as simple as a shoutout or formal letter/award. Compensation is great, but in jobs where people like their work, money is generally not as effective a motivator as praise.*

  - *When people give it their best, I have found it can be infectious and helps the whole team. Competing is a very natural instinct for humans, and success and winning are also great motivators.*

- Be fair and ethical.

  - *A big game-playing taboo is cheating, which is just as unacceptable in a work environment, so it is important to work with honour.*

- Leave it on the field.

  - *One should "play the game" and put it all out there, but once the game finishes, you need to let it go and move on to the next thing. This means don't bring your work home. It is important to have balance, which allows you to be refreshed.*

  - *Don't hold a grudge against someone who perhaps did better than you or who called you out on something (like a referee). Moving on is important for the next time you need to work with someone.*

  - *In short, take Moore's Third Law to heart: it's just a game—don't take it personally.*

Now let's take this law and see how you as a manager can apply it to the workplace:

1. Try to use sports analogies for people. It's natural, since we already call departments and groups of people working together "teams." If you draw on team dynamics, I have used the analogy of a rowing team to demonstrate how important it is that everyone works or "strokes" in the same way, at the same pace. It is catastrophic for one person to row at their own pace in a boat with many rowers.

   One of my favorite sports analogies for our work life is comparing big activities or projects to a marathon. You can discuss the importance of training and preparation in this analogy; for example, marathoners don't just wake up one morning and say, "I think I will run 26.2 miles today." One needs to pace oneself in a marathon. You will be exerting yourself for a long time, and it's crucial to have reserves for the end of the race. In all races, there is a point where you feel like you hit the wall, but perseverance and focus will help you get through that barrier.

2. Make activities at work a competition. As I discussed before, we have been competing since childhood, and it comes naturally to most of us. I do appreciate that competition is not for everyone and in more recent times there has been greater awareness that it can create undue stress, so it must be done with all participants feeling comfortable. Setting up a game for a prize and (most important) for bragging rights for some job or task can be very engaging for the team.

   Early in my life, I worked as a shift supervisor at a grocery store stocking shelves. It was a night shift, so productivity could easily slide. The expectation for each worker was to be able to open, price, and stock 40 boxes of merchandise per hour. For an eight-hour shift, that was 320 boxes per person. At one point, we were barely handling 200 per person on a shift, so I devised a game we could play. The other members of the team would always pay for breakfast for the person with the best productivity for a shift, since we always went for breakfast after the shift. We usually had four people including me on the team so things weren't very punitive, and anyone could opt out of the game. It was amazing how successful it was. Everyone loved the bragging rights that they were the fastest that night, and breakfast always tasted better when it was free. Within a year we would constantly have box counts above 320 per person per shift or, as the company viewed it, 100 percent productivity.

3.   Ensure that you as the manager have clearly explained to your workforce what the goal is and that they know what the status is at any given moment. As in a hockey game, the goal is to make more goals than the other team. Interestingly, each team member can also have an individual goal; for example, the goalie wants to have the lowest goals-per-game average, a forward wants to have the most goals and assists, and a defenceman cares about their plus/minus number.

   If you keep a workforce clear about what they are working towards and they can see their progress against those goals, your team is more likely to be motivated and focused.

4.   Make sure that failing isn't the end of the world. Even if people are really pushing themselves and trying their best, occasionally they will fail. When I taught five-year-olds how to skate, the first few lessons always involved learning how to fall. Falling will always happen in skating, so you might as well get comfortable with it and learn to get up and keep going. So, in work a manager

needs to support someone who has failed. Let them get up, learn from the mistake, and try again.

A work colleague once said something very profound to me in the middle of my career. Some coworkers and I were having a heated debate about the importance of what we were doing and how it was very life-changing. Heavy stuff. At the peak of this rather frenzied discussion, another colleague who had been observing looked at us and said, "If a book was ever written on the history of the world, what we are doing at this moment will not even be a period."

I had to think about this for a minute, but they sure helped me put some perspective on our discussion. They were absolutely right: I was not creating the cure for cancer or splitting an atom—either of which might merit a whole sentence—but our discussion certainly didn't, especially in the context of the four billion years of the earth's existence. Interestingly this advice had a very calming effect on me once I put things into perspective.

So, let's just play the game to our best ability and have some fun along the way.

Moore's Fourth Law

Shit Happens,

Get Over It

reflected a lot on the sequence in which I would order my list of Moore's Laws. I considered several factors, such as each law's:

- impact on the team and organization;

- number of times when it is applicable; and

- ability to be mitigated and by what.

The Fourth Law—shit happens, get over it—definitely made the top four, since outside forces always seem to wreak havoc on our lives. (Have you ever noticed they seem to interfere at the most inopportune times, too?)

Usually, it's easy to recognize when this law applies—usually someone is signaling disbelief in their eyes or throwing an expressive hand gesture in the air. Yes, when shit happens, it not only can be disruptive but also incredibly stressful. Being a good manager means that if shit—however you define it—happens to you or one of your team members, you should address it calmly and thoughtfully. It really helps a team to get back on track if the situation can be addressed, dealt with, learned from—and then moved on from.

As implied by the S-word in this law, the event in focus is usually disruptive and will vary in impact. It is important, though, to analyse the situation methodically before dismissing things by quoting this law. Moore's Fourth Law is not a "get out of jail free" card.

I have found a good general method for handling unexpected situations or "events" whose steps are:

1. Assess and collect data of the impact of the event.

   My first priority is always, Was anyone hurt? Injuries must be dealt with before anything else. Ensuring your team has been trained with the necessary first aid skills and safety procedures is essential. I have worked in field operations where hydrogen sulphide gas (H_2S) is always a risk, a deadly one if you do not react properly. (I probably should mention that for most of my life, I have been involved with processing products that generally burn or explode.) To me, the worst situation in these scenarios occurs when other individuals, who mean well but are not trained, try to assist and then get injured. A single mishandled gas leak has the potential to be fatal for the untrained (however well-meaning).

When I was a teenager, we had just moved to a trailer park near the Bruce Nuclear power station, a family business in Ontario. One day, the septic tank at the business was blocked, and two of the sons went to fix it. The first brother went into the tank with no safety equipment and was overcome by methane fumes. The second saw him collapse and immediately jumped down to save him. The tragic result of this situation was that the family lost two of its sons that day. We were a very close community, and it was truly a surreal event. It was even more frustrating, since most of the people in our community worked at the plant and already knew the safety procedures for entering enclosed spaces where gas is present.

Once you address safety, collect the data pertaining to the physical situation

2.   Ask, What is the operation status of the environment?

Can we or can we not operate or perform the work, and how important is each impacted area? What are the financial impacts to the organization? The answers to these questions give us the ability to assign a priority to the event.

3.   Develop a plan to bring the situation back to a normal mode.

This can be a long and multistep process or a quick fix. It might be able to be addressed in the short term with a workaround or a backup. The important thing is to create the plan and start working on it.

4. Collect as much information as possible about the event. Was anything changed leading up to it?

    This data collection is required for the root cause analysis phase of dealing with the event and learning from it. I won't discuss problem analysis further, since most organizations have good procedures in place. There are also many excellent books on this subject.

    I will just add one point that has always been important to me in this exercise. I like to ask the question "Why?" five times. That means that, for every answer I am given for why something happened, I respond "Why?" to that answer. Usually by the fifth "why," we are getting to the true root of the situation.

5. Summarize the event with a "lessons learnt" document and make sure to share it with others.

    A great example of this process is the review that Transport Canada does for all airplane accidents. The company posts them in a monthly update, and I always spent time reviewing each situation and how the recommendations made me aware of both potential problems and how to handle them properly.

When you manage situations using these regimented steps, you'll find that many disruptive events are preventable. If your organization learns from them and implements new procedures, there likely will be fewer such situations to deal with in the future. More important, you don't just let things happen and learn nothing to prevent them from happening again. As the famous saying goes (credited to the philosopher and essayist George Santayana), "Those who cannot remember the past are condemned to repeat it."

Unfortunately, some things in life are unpredictable or are very difficult to avoid, so how does a good manager deal with situations and feelings their team will experience? Here are a few ways I have used to deal with them:

1. Why does everyone think things happen only to them?

    We all go through that valley of despair when you feel you can't do anything right, something unforeseen always happens. As a manager you must help people understand there is no conspiracy theory and I often find, pointing out things recently that have gone well, changes a person's perspective on the situation. Positive thinking is very important to bringing a person out of this state.

2. Be prepared. Have contingencies.

    Although some things can't be foreseen, many can, if you just spend time thinking about possible scenarios. As an example, let's use a family road trip. I frequently took the family down to Edmonton or Calgary from Fort McMurray while I was working at Suncor. It is a long and sparsely populated journey (over four hours). So, before we started, I would go through a checklist of sorts that would identify what we needed to have in the car in case of a mechanical breakdown, an accident, or an in-car illness on the way. We put supplies in the car, charged our phones fully, and told others about our plans and expected arrival time. These were important preparations for when we were driving in Alberta winters, when temperatures can drop to minus 30. Adjust as needed in your life as a manager.

3. Keep calm to reduce stress, which makes a difference in your ability to think.

    Nothing ever gets fixed by yelling at it or kicking it, although I must admit I may have done both, particularly with some of the clunkers I drove when I was young. This advice may sound silly, but counting to 10 really can help you overcome that initial reaction. In major situations when I have the luxury of time, I also sleep on things, because alternatives frequently come to me the next day.

4. Nothing is worth losing your life.

My favorite illustration of this point occurred while I was flying. My brother and I had to check out our airplane after its annual inspection—and quickly, since we needed to fly to our company's oil fields in Saskatchewan. I was the pilot and he was the copilot. We quickly did our ground checkout and jumped into the plane to do a final flight checkout. After completing the startup and taxiing to the active runway, my brother looked down at his feet and picked up a bolt that was lying on the floor of the plane. Well, we just looked at each other and both thought, Where did that come from? I'm not sure about you, but a bolt in a small plane is a big deal. For me as a pilot, it immediately calls to mind the great saying, "Better to be a pilot on the ground wishing he was in the air than a pilot in the air wishing he was on the ground."

As you can guess, we turned around, parked the plane, and notified our mechanic that we needed the plane inspected again due to this mysterious bolt. Everything worked out fine in the end, but we never did find out where that bolt came from. (We finally decided that it must have been a spare the mechanic had dropped.)

So, shit will happen, and we must be prepared to deal with it and move on. In the end, humor is a great healer and helps the moving-on process. It is amazing how much better you feel when you can laugh about something. Sure, maybe you won't laugh right away, but sometimes thinking about how ridiculous the event was can help you get some perspective.

It also helps if you can think of ways things could have been worse. Doing so allows you to pat yourself on the back for reacting well or just thinking that you had a little good luck and that maybe this disruption happened at a good time, all things considered.

A lot of times, I have seen some preventative measure put in place that stopped the problem from becoming a catastrophe—a great shoutout for the value of doing root cause analysis for each incident you experience and implementing the recommendations that arise from your evaluation.

Moore's Fifth Law

Communicate, Don't Disseminate

Suncor Energy had a great annual process where leaders had to have a discussion with an employee who was once removed from the leader's position. So, I would schedule a meeting with all my managers' direct reports, and in turn I would meet with my own leader's manager. The structure of the meeting was to get to know them and their career aspirations and help them with long-term planning for their roles and responsibilities. I believe my record for a single year was 127 meetings, and I really enjoyed discussing with everyone their perceptions of themselves and the organization. Due to the many discussions I had some years, my assistant had to plan meetings every month; otherwise, I could never get through them all. This worked out well, since I was constantly getting a pulse on people's feelings and how changes or new directions were affecting them. I highly recommend this practice to all managers.

Over time I started to notice differences between employees' interpretations of key messages that were presented to the staff and the true direction or intent behind what our department and the company had said. This split presented an opportunity to improve the organization's alignment, so I formalized my "management once removed" (MOR) meetings to have time to discuss current messages being floated. Although most people did get the general intent, it was in the details that things would differ. After a year of this process, I came away with the understanding that all we were doing was disseminating information to people. What we were not doing was communicating well.

What Is Communication Versus Dissemination?

When I discussed this observation with peers, their immediate response was "Aren't communicating and disseminating the same thing?" I believe they are entirely different. To me, communication is the successful transmission of a thought or idea from one person to another, "success" meaning that the message was interpreted with 100 percent accuracy.

This belief was further clarified by a leadership course I attended that discussed three key elements of communication, which are:

- *What we think*

- *What we say*

- *What they hear*

When we show the information that is being communicated as a bubble, as shown in the illustration below, only one zone of the information is aligned or correct. When we join all three elements in overlapping bubbles, evidence suggests that as much as 98 percent of communication results in some degree of misunderstanding of its original intent. Many of us feel that way about our partners, and it can make for a lively conversation at home when you bring up this topic. In fact, my wife thinks that 98 percent is too low, and that 99 percent is only slightly more accurate!

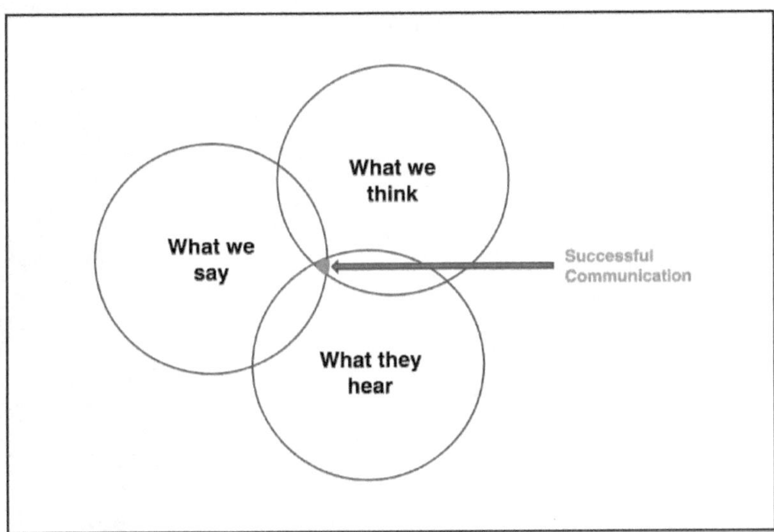

Dissemination is merely the transmission of thoughts or ideas with no confirmation of receipt or understanding on the part of the audience. We merely disseminate information through announcements, presentations, and media and even in discussions—we are frequently not communicating. Many of these processes lack confirmation that the audience successfully received, fully understood, or interpreted the idea or message.

Being a successful manager means you must do a much better job of communicating your ideas unambiguously if you want team alignment. Here are some tools I implement that aim to transmit information clearly and without ambiguity.

The KISS Principle

You may be familiar with this acronym for "Keep It Simple, Stupid."

I used to think that complexity of thought signaled intelligence, but over the years it was frustrating to discover that many solutions or ideas I had created or worked on just weren't being understood. It is common to have to say things many times for communication to really sink in, but when ideas are made complicated, people generally have too many chances to take the idea and develop it in an unintended direction. I believe now that the most difficult thing to do is to show something complex very simply. That is true genius.

A good example of when I have used the KISS principle occurred when I had to explain the implementation of an enterprise resource system (or ERP) at Suncor. For those of you in the IT field, you understand the experience of trying to explain what an ERP system really does and what its benefits are. Sure, you can talk like a rocket scientist on the subject, but few listeners can stay attentive for the whole conversation.

Prior to our ERP implementation, we were like most large organizations whose IT systems grew out of opportunities to automate manually intensive systems like finance, materials management, maintenance planning, loss control, HR, and others. Over time, the organization needed to share the information collected by all the different systems. As those needs arose, we in IT were commissioned to create interfaces to enable that sharing of information among systems. In addition, with expansion, the company added more systems with requirements to share newly created information, thereby creating further need for more interfaces.

What soon became painfully obvious was the exponential growth of the maintenance work needed to ensure the proper interdependencies and the accuracy and up-to-dateness of data. One of our team members created a master diagram of all the systems, including the flows of information through interfaces among them. The lines looked like a mass of spaghetti, only less organized; the diagram was difficult to read and understand. Our CIO at the time reviewed this diagram during a planning meeting and said, "This is becoming gridlocked." What a great way to describe the out-of-control evolution of disparate systems that must be synchronized and what happens when too many interdependencies create an almost impossible workload, especially when updates and changes are needed. Basically, controlling this sort of gridlock, complete with interdependencies and sometimes complicated relationships, is what ERP systems were made for.

An ERP system might be too technically complex to be reduced to easy explanations, but when our IT department used the term "gridlock," it instantly registered with leaders and employees—and they understood quickly why the company needed an ERP platform for efficient and effective management of data. A classic example of the effectiveness of the KISS principle.

Another small example of KISS occurred during a discussion with the executive team on the benefits of using an ERP software called SAP. A senior vice president said to me, "I've heard that SAP is very flexible, but I've also heard that once it is installed, it's very difficult to change things. Which is true?"

It was a very good question. Part of good communication is speaking to people in terms they easily understand and that can be done very effectively with analogies. After giving his question some thought, I came up with the analogy that SAP was like cement. When you use wet cement to build a foundation, you can design any shape or size that the cement will conform to. Wet cement is very flexible for creating what you need. But what happens once you pour the cement and it hardens? In that state, just try to change what it looks like. You will find it takes a significant amount of effort to modify that shape.

This analogy—SAP as cement—really made sense to him, and I was pleased how many people I could use this analogy with to provide a better understanding of the software and why configuring it right at the beginning was critical.

Confirm With Feedback

Have you ever noticed that in conversation with others, people commonly start thinking of a response even before the other person has finished speaking? I have been guilty as charged on many occasions for doing that exact thing. It's a bad habit and one that contributes to lack of communication, because the speaker has not successfully conveyed their idea, since the other person has really stopped listening.

The best way to ensure information is transferred successfully is through feedback. It's important for managers to avoid misunderstandings, so simply asking "What did I just say?" or saying "Tell me in your own words how you would explain this" can head off a lot of misinterpretations.

When receiving information from someone, it is also good practice to play back what someone has said in your own words prior to your response. I normally start my response with, *"This is what I think you said."* As an example of this practice, early in my career, I had to meet with a vice president of the upgrading plant. He was truly an inspiration for his obvious focus on our conversation. You could tell by his amazing degree of eye contact and how he used a series of questions to ensure his complete understanding of what I was saying. For me, knowing I was being listened to was incredibly motivating, and I have tried to instill that same focus in my own people.

Here's another tip. When going into a meeting, put your cell phone on silent. Doing so will prevent you from being distracted, and people will know they are important to you.

Another great way to ensure others understand the material is to have them teach it. Throughout my career, I have had to teach many subjects, put on a seminar, or present reports. You really internalize the material when you have to play it back and have people ask questions on it.

Having someone be a trainer isn't the only way of "teaching"; create subject matter experts and give them the opportunity to present the material. This will ensure you have consistency in spreading messages throughout the organization.

Emotional Connection Is Powerful for Memory Retention

Do you remember what you were doing when 9/11 happened, or, if you happen to be as old as I am, when Neil Armstrong first walked on the moon? Even though I was only eight when he did that, it is as clear a memory as if it was yesterday. Another interesting phenomenon I experience is that I remember questions on a test I got wrong much more than the ones I got right. Why? Because I usually got very mad with myself, particularly when it was something silly like I misread the question.

I believe that emotions are linked to memory. If you want someone to remember something and have it be core to their being, it has to be connected to some feeling. As a manager, you must bring that emotion to bear on subjects or actions. Any emotion (humor, anger, excitement, etc.) will work, and it's your role to use the right one.

For additional information on this subject, I have found that the sales thought leader Sharon-Drew Morgen (who goes by Sharon-Drew) has some very good thoughts and is published on this challenge. A good link to get started is her blog post, "Bridging the Gap Between What's Seen and What's Heard," available (at least as of late 2024) at https://sharon-drew.com/bridging-the-gap-between-whats-said-and-whats-heard.

In the end, a manager must be a good communicator, not a disseminator of information. Your team needs it to be able to work together as sharing and understanding that information with the same context, will create an effective workforce.

Moore's Sixth Law

Be Consistent

Human nature is drawn to routine. Predictability is a good thing in many aspects of life. Sure, a surprise or two and spontaneity can be refreshing, but a constant barrage of disruptions is draining. The more important downside of constantly being interrupted or changing your plans is that it generally leads to what I call "activity thrashing." Constant stops and starts result in lost productivity, because it takes time to reset and engage in new activities.

In the work environment, a key element to enable routine is having consistency in your strategy, goals, priorities, and activities. All those elements do need change and updates, but the frequency of that change is important to an organization and its people so that we can provide periods of when activities are in a consistent steady state. The timelines for changing strategies, goals, priorities, and activities are very different and it's worth giving you a target for each.

My recommendation for timing strategic changes is that updates or major shifts should occur every three to five years. This interval primarily relies on the idea that this is the length of time a strategy or direction needs to be implemented before you have the hindsight and experience to evaluate its success or lack thereof.

Goals should be annual milestones. The big factor is not to have too many of them. They need to show clearly how you are working towards achieving the strategy. This simple check will allow your team to have different individual goals while remaining consistent with the strategy and thus minimizing opposing agendas in your team.

Priorities and activities are more of a monthly review. Anything briefer and your organization will spend more time jumping from one priority to another than completing the work.

As a manager, you enable your team by delivering your messages consistently. Being consistent builds trust and credibility in your leadership, whereas being inconsistent leads to the eventuality that someone will catch you making contradictory statements, creating confusion and eroding trust. You may think it's okay to give different directions or information to people in order to motivate them and avoid conflict. This is, however, dangerous and the consequence of people spotting discrepancies in your words and practices is even worse than if you just gave them the same information twice.

I have always believed that everybody finds out all information, particularly anything you try to keep secret. Here are three areas where secrets get outed all the time—so it's important to be consistent in your practices just in case the information does get out.

Salaries. It is drilled into us as managers that you never disclose another person's salary, which is a breach of confidentiality. Funny thing, though: people like to talk and very often share salary information. If you as a manager don't believe that all people were treated fairly and equitably, then you're in a difficult position when people find there are perceived (and probably true) inequalities of treatment (bonus distribution, raises, etc.). These differences have the potential to leave you perceived as hiding information or, worse, playing favorites. When that happens, trust in you just flies out the window.

Organizational changes. This includes promotions and, more important, those who don't get a job or promotion. The appropriate process or action is to use common sense, of course, but this is still worth calling out. You should always meet or have a discussion with the individuals who didn't get the job *before* you meet with the person you are giving it to. You may tell a person not to discuss a promotion they are getting, but information always seems to get out. Be careful, because a tricky situation can arise when you offer someone a position and they don't accept it. That would be a problem if you already told the next candidate they didn't get the role. In those situations, getting confirmation of acceptance has to be done first, then you need to quickly inform the other candidates they didn't get the role. This advice about consistency may itself sound inconsistent—tell the winning candidate first, or the runners-up who didn't get the job? The key point is that speed and effective communication are warranted with all candidates to avoid creating that discontent that can develop when a person doesn't get the role and, worse, hears the news from someone other than the hiring manager. It makes them believe that you didn't have the nerve to give them the bad news yourself. Another option is to inform all but the chosen and alternative candidates that they did not get the role. Then deal quickly with accepting and rejecting the finalists, preferably on the same day. It is always better to hear the news from the hiring manager.

Acquisitions or mergers. In my leadership roles, I have been involved with several acquisitions and one merger where, during the due diligence phase, secrecy was critical, particularly since the companies were publicly traded. This is when it is critical to be consistent with discussing your activities. A good way to think about secrets is, *"If you tell even one person, it's not a secret anymore."* All communication you have on these topics should be extremely brief. The longer you discuss something, the more likely you are to disclose information inappropriately.

In the rare cases when you find it is appropriate to be inconsistent and you give different messages to different areas in the workplace, be very careful. I like to classify this information as "deviations from the base case." You may need to have several deviations depending on the group or team. But if this happens, be very sure you are repeating the same deviation to the same group. Unless you are very clear with people that a particular situation is a special case, deviations are like setting a precedent in court. Once a deviation occurs, it will be cited forever, and no one will let you forget it.

More important, your credibility and trustworthiness will forever be in doubt. I really like to keep things simple, and my default is that it's best not to say anything at all. If pressed, a simple explanation for those who press you on a subject is that you cannot say anything now, but at the appropriate time we will have a full discussion. Asking members of your team to do something without an explanation should be okay if you have a good relationship with your people.

Another element of being consistent is following through on your commitments, activities, and promises. Some people might have a different perspective on follow-ups and say they are unrelated to consistency. I suppose one could argue that a person who never completes a job or does poor work is exhibiting consistent behaviour. True, but we are trying to build on positive attributes and work abilities in this book, so let's align on that perspective.

So, the bottom line is that teams need consistency and follow-through, because it's important from an efficiency perspective to have confidence that a person on their team will deliver on a commitment when they said they would. With complex work, you rely on having that piece of the puzzle to continue to the next step. Having quality work delivered as expected creates an effective team.

In summary, *consistency decreases confusion and builds solid relationships for all team members*. Management and job execution should be built on general principles and common sense. You should feel that if everyone applies them, they will be consistent.

Moore's Seventh Law

ACE
(Argue, Consent, Execute)

The seventh law—argue, consent, execute (ACE)—really speaks to execution within a team and how to create effective buy-in for a direction we want to go in.

I have seen groups of people executing decisions in this manner for a long time, but the first time I heard it defined so succinctly was when I worked for the networking company Ungermann-Bass in the early 1990s. Most people today wouldn't even know of that company, but in the 1980s and 1990s, it was the leader in computer networking and one of the first companies to sell fiber optic technology. Because this organization was heavily staffed with creative engineers and pioneered many computer network technologies, creative differences would arise often.

ACE builds on the premise of being one team with one plan and executing it together. A great example of this would be an eight-person rowing team. You can imagine that if each rower in the boat decided to row at the pace they want, conflict or clashes with the oars would ensue and you wouldn't go very fast, that's for sure. But if they all stroke at the pace set by the coxswain, the team is synchronized and the boat glides through the water, almost effortlessly reaching maximum speed.

ACE is a good process for achieving the goal of working together with three simple steps.

Step 1: Argue

If you want a team to get behind a decision, it's best to have a forum where people can express their thoughts and concerns collaboratively. This may sound easy but takes a long time to do, because people are usually skeptical or bashful and don't want to be ostracized.

Establish that the arguing phase is to ensure that all ideas and perspectives get a chance to be reviewed and that it is a safe zone where no suggestion is too silly. As I noted earlier in the book, "Given the same information, reasonable people come up with the same result or answer." But "given the same information" is not a simple premise, because the same information is not necessarily shared. What if you base your decision on the knowledge you have of people's history or biases? Are you sharing all your personal experiences when you made a similar decision, and it didn't go well?

It's easy to look at an idea and say, "We did that 10 years ago, and it failed miserably." Sometimes the timing of an idea is important, which should be considered before the group dismisses it for having failed at another time.

A good example is the touchscreen technology for computer monitors. When I was at Hewlett Packard in the 1980s, the company introduced the HP-150 personal computer with touchscreen capability. It wasn't the first application of touchscreens, but it was the first commercially available computer to use them. It was big and bulky, with only (as I remember) a nine-inch screen. HP used a beam technology that detected where you pointed at on the screen. The resolution was not very good, and the HP-150 had few applications that used the technology. Eventually it was scrapped. So imagine being the engineer suggesting, years later, a new touchscreen to a manager who was on the original HP-150 project. That engineer would probably have been shot down immediately.

Fast-forward to today, and touchscreens on computers and phones are pervasive. The technology changed and improved, applications became easier to use, and voilà, touchscreens became viable. In fact, it's hard now to remember when we didn't have them, and we can't imagine how difficult using many of today's applications would be without them.

So: argue productively. A bad idea twenty years ago might be a perfect idea for this moment in time.

Step 2: Consent

Although I am sure there are many ways to consent on a decision, the most effective methods I have used are:

Leadership decision. Many situations cannot be resolved by consensus. Someone has to make a call, after, it is hoped, they have solicited input from trusted sources. The conditions for a leadership decision primarily fall into three categories:

1. *Accountability*. It is clear by the decision that a single person must take responsibility and be the one others can go to for clarification and understanding of why something was done.

2. *Timing or speed.* Many times, a quick decision is needed to avert a greater disaster or major impact for an organization. If you must get several people together to agree on a course of action, it can be too late. In these situations, it is important that it is very clear who has the authority to make that decision, because lower levels in the organization may not have the information that the manager has. You cannot have a line supervisor shutting down the plant if they are running low on inventory, since they may not know that a shipment is eight hours away.

3. *Even split.* Occasionally two choices emerge that have equal support within the group. The leader is then responsible for breaking the tie. (The US Senate works this way, whereby if 50% of the Senate supports a legislative bill and the other 50% rejects it, then the US Vice President acts as the president of the Senate and breaks the tie.)

Majority vote. As the name suggests, a group of people are given a vote on a motion or idea, with a simple yes/no or a selection of alternatives, and they must pick one. This setup works best when the vote leads to a decisive majority on one side or the other; when the vote becomes close, it's generally a good idea to revert to leadership.

Scoring system. At first this sounds like the easiest way to make decisions. But not so fast, my young apprentice. Scoring systems have several criteria to be evaluated and given points or a score for a result or value. The weight of each element is the real magic in a great scoring system that delivers the best results. For clarification, if one element on a choice is its price and you need to score it out of 10, does only 1 option score a 10, then the next gets a 9, and so on? Or do you have a range, with all solutions that are with 10 percent get 10, then the next group that is 10 percent lower or higher gets a 9. Does price have the same weight as ease of use? If you are purchasing a product or service and you want to evaluate the reliability of the product or service, how would you score the difference, on complaints, failures etc.? I'm sure your head is spinning now, and did those last sentences even make sense to you.

A cute story of something we tried to score at Suncor was the impact of technology outages at the company. This was necessary for our journey to have a service level agreement and balance the cost of service against the loss of production or level of safety required. If we had just used one criterion—normally how long an outage lasted—it would become a challenge quickly, since an organization must consider many more factors than just outage length. Here are just some of them:

- *Time of day of the outage;*

- *How many services were impacted; and*

- *How many people the outage affected.*

Well, after many discussions we agreed to develop a score for each outage by multiplying how critical an application was (as measured by number of users) as either a "prime time" (during regular work hours) or "nonprime time" (outside of regular work hours) value and by the number of minutes. Every application affected by an outage would have a score and need to be added up as a cumulative effect. This resulted in crazy score numbers, but these scores gave us an order of magnitude of the effect on the company. One of my managers then asked, "Well, what is the unit of measurement? Minutes, users, dollars?" None of these actually, but just telling people a seemingly random number for the severity of their outage would be confusing, so after a little bit of thought, I came up with "gerstupnick."

Completely ridiculous in many ways and not even a word, but it was hilarious to see people's reactions. The point was to clarify for people that the score summed up many factors, each weighted differently to show the impact on the company. The value in this situation was to see the trend, not the absolute number.

The last factor you should be careful of in scoring is the score's ability to skew the outcome in a specific direction. Weighting incorrectly tends to make a criterion more important than it really should be. All these things need to be understood before you go down the scoring rabbit hole.

Step 3: Execute

Execution would seem to be the easy step of the three—argue, consent, execute—but many times I have worked through the ACE process and walked out of a meeting only to find later that we didn't really have complete agreement and that some individuals were still pursuing their own ideas or undermining the work to the point of sabotaging what we were executing.

Another way of looking at the execution phase and the criticality of ensuring that everyone is executing the same thing would be to use flying as an analogy. At flight school you are taught that there can only be one pilot in command. A joke among pilots is, "What is the most dangerous time for a pilot in a four-seater plane?" The answer: "When the other three seats are occupied by flight instructors!"

Can you imagine being at a critical step in piloting a plane, like landing, and all of a sudden you have three people telling you what you should do next? In my experience, even when I had another pilot beside me and they broke my checklist routine, it became difficult to get back on track without potentially missing a step. Pilots have an understanding that a single person is in control until another pilot issues the command, "I HAVE CONTROL." This is usually done by a more experienced pilot and that is generally agreed to before you start your flight. This simple procedure is clear and concise and the safest way to fly.

The bottom line is, once a decision is made, everyone complies, so go out there and ACE it.

Moore's Eighth Law

MBWA
(Management by Wandering Around)

MBWA, or "management by wandering around," was a practice I embraced that evolved from the HP Way, the management philosophy at Hewlett Packard. When I worked for HP in the 1980s, it had a strong bootcamp that really immersed you in the culture of the organization. Many of the management principles and core values I learned from HP have been gems of wisdom. *The HP Way*, by Dave Packard, HP's cofounder, is a great book and easy to read.[1] I highly recommend that you take the time to familiarize yourself with it and the company's founding principles. For me, it was always special to chat with someone who had interacted with Dave Packard directly. He was truly an amazing manager and an inspiration to his people. I think the most memorable part of the stories I used to hear was that he had tremendous humility and genuinely appreciated others' contributions.

MBWA is another concept that isn't new, and many good leaders have incorporated it into their style without giving it much thought. The reason I like to call MBWA one of my laws of management is that this technique enabled me to improve my interactions with people in the organization. As I've stated before, if you are not interested in people, don't get into management.

"Wandering" rather than, say, "walking" is key to describing this practice. The word has an element of whimsicality, almost randomness. If you drop into someone's cubicle or office only to get a status update on an escalation, then you will miss the opportunity to learn other things you didn't know. What's more, showing up only during crises can set up, in people's minds, negative associations about their interactions with you. As proof of that, I had a couple of years that were crazy busy, and it felt like I was jumping from one fire to another. A really good employee I had worked with for years was

---

1   David Packard, *The HP Way: How Bill Hewlett and I Built Our Company* (Harper Collins, 1995).

in my office one day giving me an update on a critical system outage. When we finished the discussion, he casually mentioned, "Gee Paul, it's a shame I only see you when something bad is going on." Wow, even as a joke that hit me like a ton of bricks. Had my management style deteriorated to the point where I was only involved with the negatives? I felt as if I must have been the Grim Reaper to many of my people who didn't know me well. I decided right then to change how I interacted with people and made sure to inject praise and comments of general interest into conversations to create more balanced interactions.

So, how do you embark on the practice of "management by wandering around"? A simple one is never to drink your coffee in your office. Take the time to go to the coffee station or water cooler, heck, even make a pot of coffee yourself. You will easily strike up a conversation or two with people in that area.

Try to time walking around the halls five to 10 minutes before the hour. When meetings start on the hour, usually a few people arrive early to get ready for the meeting. By poking your head into a meeting before it starts to see what's going on, you show that you are interested.

Go to another floor just to walk around the corridors. Chances are a couple of people are having a discussion in an open area. Don't be afraid to come up and engage with them.

An offshoot of MBWA is having an open-door policy. Give yourself an occasional open window of time, with no formal meetings scheduled, and use it for general admin work or catch-up if nobody drops by. Your open door tells people you have time and that they can drop by to discuss things informally. My teams knew that I liked to come in early to prepare for the day's activities. I generally preferred not to schedule meetings until 9:00 a.m., so from 7:00

a.m. (when I generally got into the office) to 9:00 a.m., I had time for discussions. It's not wandering around, but it is showing an openness to interacting with people.

It also doesn't hurt to have some candy in your office. I loved the little peppermint candies in the big tub you could buy at Costco. Perhaps they worked too well with some people, to the point where my good friend John Debleyser, my head of architecture, was an addict! Well, at least I was always up to date with the direction our technology was headed.

In the end, physical presence in a casual atmosphere is the best for open, honest feedback. Humans are very tactile and pick up on body language and mannerisms that just can't be conveyed over the phone or, worse, in an email. Many people want to feel a connection to people they work with. We do spend a significant portion of our lives at work, so why shouldn't it be comfortable?

If you are able to achieve effective MBWA, the benefits can be summarized as follows. Professionally you get to:

- Understand current challenges, hot off the press, as it were;

- Hear about items that usually aren't brought up in status meetings, but through your experience or understanding of the bigger picture are themselves significant and might have major effects;

- Sometimes just listen to someone explain a current problem, which can allow them to solve the problem themselves. Just the process of explaining things to another person seems to spur your own analysis and lead you to think of things you may have overlooked. Some probing questions in your effort to seek to understand doesn't hurt either;

- Clear up any misinterpretations or misunderstandings; and

- Learn about friction points within teams and in their interactions with others.

Personal connections should be kept to a level that people desire. It's important that managers do not pry into people's personal lives. Personal privacy and rights are very important in today's world.

- You can be a good listener, which can give you a greater understanding of what motivates people and what's important to them. Most people don't want you to solve their problems, but it feels good just to get things off their chest.

- Get an understanding if people have other stresses or distractions in their lives. A sickness in the family is very disruptive today. Most people's lives are incredibly busy, and unexpected events are difficult to handle.

- Showing interest or empathy for people generates loyalty, and they will be more apt to give that extra effort when you need it.

The bottom line is that you will gain a better understanding of what goes on in your organization, and you will be viewed as a leader, not just as a manager.

Moore's Ninth Law

Work to Live, Don't Live to Work

I've always liked the saying "Work to live, don't live to work" due to its simplicity and how you have two words, *live* and *work*, and just by reversing them in a statement, you end up with two very different meanings. Another way to look at Moore's Ninth Law is that you should have balance in your life. Easy to say, hard to achieve.

I am now close to 65 years old and must admit to having had times in my life when there was no balance and it felt as if I was just working, building a career, putting in those extra hours and really not doing much else. But when I look back at my life, those times are not the first things I remember. Rather it's the amazing Disney vacations we had, or celebrating special events with friends and family, or motorcycle trips through the mountains with my buddies.

For me, living also involved having a bucket list or personal goals for which I needed to put a plan in place to achieve them. Things like learning to fly a plane and breaking my personal best time in a triathlon were major achievements, and they were even more important due to the time and dedication it took to achieve them. I have become aware that in life, the journey is more important than the destination. Those activities were not possible without working and having the income to indulge in them, and that is a big reason why I worked.

The first person to really stress the work-life balance concept to me was a great manager I had at Suncor. Doug Pelton was trying to hire me and move to Fort McMurray, Alberta. The thought of moving back to the remote northern community wasn't at the top of my to-do list and I had a couple of other prospects that were interesting but required me to live on a plane, something that I had already been doing for 10 years and, quite frankly, I was getting tired and burned out.

He stressed in my interview that the oil sands plant was more like a family, and it was a great place to engage in family activities, all of which were possible due to the generous vacation and personal time off. Well, I drank the Kool-Aid and joined Suncor, which was one of the best career decisions I ever made.

Not only did my career grow, but the community atmosphere was amazing. We created a Saturday morning running club and as long as it was warmer than minus 25 degrees, we ran. Personally, I thought the coffee at Tim Horton's after the run was usually the biggest reason I got out of bed to brave the cold winter runs. But even something as simple as the coffee shop was great, and you couldn't finish a coffee without having a dozen conversations with friends and work colleagues. Even our executive VP, Mike Asher, would stop by the table to shoot the breeze. It was through those interactions that Mike recruited me to be a board member for the Arctic Winter Games that Fort McMurray hosted in 2004.

What an amazing experience, not just because athletes around the world were coming but also due to the fact that approximately 20 percent of Fort McMurray's population were volunteers—a stat I think is the highest I have ever seen for a community event.

So, why should you believe that working to live rather than living to work is a good perspective for you to have as a person and as a manager? I have found that good work-life balance provides the following benefits:

You can recharge your batteries.

- Doing the same tasks, always living in a high stress or crisis environment, takes a toll on your mental and physical health. I always experienced a strange pattern when I went on vacation. The first week, I always seemed to be recovering from some cold or flu that I just got when I started the vacation. I eventually realized that I was burning the candle at both ends to wrap up my work activities and prep the team for what was required during my absence. When I finally got to rest, my immune system was so low, I caught whatever was going around at the time.

Similarly, you can't keep pushing yourself without expecting a loss in productivity, errors in judgement or decision-making, and generally having less patience with people, even becoming quite irritable at times.

Taking some time away allows you to relax your mind. This doesn't mean you have to do nothing and sleep. Performing other activities that are not part of your normal routine has the same effect as if you were exercising different areas of the brain.

Taking a break can help you to solve problems.

- Have you ever been in a situation where you just keep looking at a problem and can't see the cause or how to fix it? As you get more frustrated, the answer seems to elude you even more. It certainly has happened to me many times in my life, and the best way I found to solve it was to walk away. This is when personal activities can help your work life, because they give the mind a distraction by letting your unconscious mind work on the problem without your realizing it.

When I was in university, one of our professors challenged us to create a computer program that performed a function with fewer instructions than he created in his own solution to the problem. The prize was substantial, an assignment mark of 110 percent. I quickly created a solution that worked but had one more step than his solution did. I must have burned my brain out for many hours over the next couple of days trying to figure out another way to solve the problem and was just getting more frustrated.

One thing I did during school was walk back and forth to the university. The trip took around 45 minutes each way, and I certainly could have done it faster with a car or bus, but I found the time relaxing and just let my mind wander. Well, on the second day of stewing on this problem during my walk, it just suddenly hit me how it could be done. I went straight to the lab, rewrote the program with two fewer instructions than the professor's solution, and gleefully collected my 110 percent.

Doing personal activities, particularly ones that allow you to accomplish something physical, can give you a feeling of accomplishment.

- I have always enjoyed managing people, and it really gives me a great sense of pride when people excel. The interesting challenge, though, is that most management activities never come with a defined completion point or finish line. Management is a constant treadmill of activity. You will always get improved productivity when you are close to finishing an activity, like in a race—you always have the energy for that last kick.

  So, the challenge is to gain that feeling and positive attitude in a role that never has that finish line. For me, engaging in personal activities outside work that had a clear completion point was a great way to maintain my mental health. These activities can be anything—building a table, finishing a puzzle, or creating a garden (complete with a waterfall, always one of my favorites). You will be amazed at how your positive vibe will permeate your work.

You communicate better with others when you can talk about things other than work.

- Have you ever been on your way to get coffee, when you see someone waving at you and coming over to talk, and you get that sinking feeling that all they want to talk about is work? It's very important, like recharging your batteries, to have a chance to discuss non-work things. If you have nothing but work in your life and that's all you are interested in, you will be that person that everyone else dreads. Having other things in your life will allow you to engage with people, help them relax, and get that much needed downtime.

You might be surprised that some of the most engaging conversations I have had in a casual setting with very senior executives were chatting about Disney vacations. It seems that everyone wants to be a kid again, and it really is a happy place.

So now that I have persuaded you that working to live is a good idea, what tools will allow better work-life balance?

- Remote tools can allow you to be with family and address work items. This is also a two-edged sword, since working remotely can lead to distractions, and you are not in the moment. The personal mobile device (we certainly can't just call it a "phone" anymore) is by far the worst for this. You almost can't go to a game or dine out without seeing more than half the people with their heads down, texting, snapping pictures, or just surfing the internet. Sure, occasionally someone is actually responding to some crisis at work, but again, let's be critical about the criteria for "critical." Would the world come to an end if you didn't respond until you had finished eating or actually watched your son or daughter score that goal?

- It's okay to set expectations for work behaviour and to lead by example. One example: no emails from 6:00 p.m. to 6:00 a.m.

Having boundaries and treating personal activities as priorities is a good thing. As a manager, you must help your team feel that it's appropriate for them too. You will be a better manager for it and, I believe, achieve that work-to-live goal.

Moore's Tenth Law

Family First

The final law, Moore's Tenth Law, is a fitting way to summarize how you should view your life, your priorities, and what really matters in the scheme of things: family first.

Your family is your support, and you are theirs. Many of us go through life thinking that they are always there for you. While this idea can give you a much-needed sense of stability, it does not give you the right to assume or take for granted this loyalty or let you reduce your commitments to them.

Do not underestimate your role in the family and the impact achieved through your engagement with them. What you might consider a minor issue or trivial matter may be the most important thing to that person.

For my oldest child, Natalie, it was her swim meets. She loved to swim and was a great competitor. One time, I was involved in some important consulting on the East Coast with very aggressive timelines and was away over 80 percent of the time. During a qualifying swim meet that year, she had an amazing race and achieved her first qualifying time to go to Provincials. Provincials happened to be during an important time at work, and I was supposed to be far off on the East Coast. I knew this achievement was very important to her, so I arrived at the job on the Monday of the week of Provincials and clearly (but nicely) informed my work team that we would be wrapping up the week by Wednesday night. My daughter was competing in her first ever Provincial tournament starting Thursday evening, and I was not going to miss it. Wednesday came and, as I had promised, I jumped on the plane in time to be home and to take my daughter to the big event. She did very well, making the top 10 in her best stroke (the backstroke) and had a great time. You feel an incredible sense of pride, particularly when your child does something for the first time. And of course there is only one first time.

A second example was my youngest, Annika, who is an amazing dancer and was wrapping up her last season with her dance troop before heading off to university. We had committed to being at her dance competition for the weekend, but I had to get back for a work meeting by Sunday evening. The team and Annika performed fabulously and, as it happens, they were selected to compete in the finals Sunday evening. This didn't happen very often, so it was clear I had to cancel my travel plans even at the last minute. This was a good decision, since Annika and her troop turned in an award-winning performance. I can't tell you how much I would have regretted not being there for that final performance.

In both instances, the people I worked with were completely supportive. Don't be afraid to be assertive and speak up about your family priorities. Sure, some don't have the same priorities and might use those times you have prioritized your family against you in a performance review or when career opportunities are available. But most people do think the same, and it's a great opportunity for them to see your values and your commitment to family. For those who do not, ask yourself one question: Do I really want to work with people with such different values?

Of course, I wouldn't be human if I hadn't been there for my family on some occasions. The one that I remember the most was early in my career when I was spending a lot of time in the arctic working on a project for the government account. Being very preoccupied, I didn't take the news that my second daughter, Samantha, was getting sick as anything serious. Unfortunately, over the evening she started to have trouble breathing and had to go to the hospital, where she was immediately diagnosed with pneumonia and had to be admitted.

You are likely to feel awfully guilty when you aren't there for critical situations.

I feel I did make it up to her when she had stomach surgery a couple of years later. In that situation, I was with her right from the pre-surgery stage and never left her side for seven days in post-op. It got to the point that only Dad was allowed to move her, since he had minimizing her pain down to a science.

Another factor we don't consider enough is that the most influential time in our lives is when we are young. That time doesn't come back, and you only get one chance at it, so stop telling yourself "I can do that thing with the family later."

So, why is family so important to humans? I have pondered that very question for many years and believe it's rooted in our need for stability. We gather strength in our lives from some of the constants. I like to think that family is our anchor to the things that allow us to achieve great things.

As a child, I felt very anchored, yet my family life was very dynamic. We moved 13 times before I finished high school and I was constantly having to make new friends and learn the ropes for each new school. It dawned upon me that a big part of my anchor was my grandparents. They were the constant in my life; they had lived in the same house in England all their married life. When we visited them, we always had dinner at two p.m., and my grandparents always ate the same food, even in a restaurant, a trait we found both endearing and ridiculous at the same time. They were content and happy, which was always like a breath of fresh air when we visited. It also gave me a sense of comfort that no matter when I could get back to their home in England, it would be the same.

It's a great exercise for each of us to think about our own anchors. If you can't come up with yours immediately, I strongly suggest putting in the effort to locate—or even create—one.

Always remember, a person who has a stable and happy family life is a productive member of the team.

The Recipe for Moore's Laws

Well, I'm sure you have been reading the laws and thinking, these make sense, no biggie, I am doing most of them already. For many of you, I believe that is correct, but I still feel these laws could make you an even better manager if you executed them differently. As an example of what I mean, Southwest Airlines never hid its strategy for being a low-cost, friendly airline. So, why was it so difficult to replicate its success when anyone could read the Southwest operating manuals?

Having strategic documents and operating procedures is not the only factor for success. I have found that it's the way you put things together that ultimately produces different outcomes. There are extra factors that each individual needs to be aware of and, with that awareness, adjust their ultimate execution of these laws. Some of those factors to be considered are the following.

Business Culture

Culture is a difficult area to define precisely, and everyone knows it is a major factor in how we interact and coexist with others. A definition of culture that is applicable to a business is:

1. Shared Attitudes, Values, and Practices

    - Within institutions or organizations, culture shapes the way of doing things. It's the set of shared norms, values, and goals that characterize how people interact and behave in the business.

    - In various fields—whether it's art, science, or technology—culture influences our approach, language, and interactions.

2. Human Knowledge and Behaviour

    - Culture is the integrated pattern of human knowledge, belief, and behaviour. It's the transmission of wisdom across generations.

    - From enlightenment to aesthetic taste, culture shapes our minds and souls.

Never underestimate the power of culture in a business. It's like a large iceberg in the sea. You can clearly see 15 percent of it, but the other 85 percent is underwater. It is also very difficult to change direction and requires a lot of effort that usually must be done gradually. In some circumstances, change might even take generations to occur.

One of my most challenging examples of that cultural shift in my career was the merger of Suncor Energy and Petro-Canada, which started in 2009 and took 18 months. A look at the assets of the two companies offered a compelling case to put these two entities together. Many synergies were possible and were achieved in subsequent years. In my leadership role during the merger, I was responsible for integrating information services between the two companies.

The role entailed working with the two organizations' IT departments, understanding their needs and delivering services efficiently and effectively. Sounds simple enough, but with two very large organizations with different cultures, the task proved to be massive. The two cultures were fundamentally as different as you could be while delivering products and services in the same field of business. One company had an entrepreneurial, startup mentality, whereas the other had a steadfast institutional origin (I will let you guess which company was which, LOL).

Even down to the department level, the organizations ran autonomously, creating systems and processes that were highly customized for their specific needs. This manifested itself in the number of business systems that were developed and supported by each company. When the total list of systems was compiled to determine how to integrate the two companies, we discovered that there were over 4,500 applications needed to run the two businesses.

The most interesting discovery was that many areas in the two companies were executing virtually the same processes, but with different applications to achieve the tasks. We found many instances of four or five applications that had over 80 percent of the same functionality. During the work to integrate the two companies, our team reduced the number of systems from 4,500 to just over 1,800, with very little loss of functionality. Culturally, though, it was a major effort to get people to change some of their operating practices and to learn new systems.

So, as a manager reading this book, you created some new ideas on how you will apply these laws into your team and organization.

Great, but don't forget to factor in some of the cultural aspects of your business to ensure that your new ideas don't meet immediate resistance. Ensure that you address the cultural issues head on and show the benefits of the changes. Yes, for some things, particularly Moore's First Law—if it's not written, it's not real—it will seem like it's unnecessary for them to do and that the overhead will decrease productivity.

I have often seen people use the lack of documentation in their work almost as a form of job security and that sometimes a company's culture rewards people who are the only one that can solve a problem. But you will convert people when they are able to resolve issues much faster with change management documentation or can clarify discrepancies in opinions about what was agreed to with a clearly written scope document.

Geography

Where people are located does dramatically affect many of the laws. It's hard to practice management by wandering around (MBWA) and hanging out at the coffee station when some of your people are in Pune, India! Some of the ideas and practices will require a physical presence. It is interesting that I have observed humans to be very tactile and rely on most of their senses when communicating with other individuals.

Don't forget that body language and tone are big ones that are difficult to read when you are remote. Impossible by text or voice, a little better with video, but you still do not get the same experience of peripheral vision through a monitor. It is quite amazing how many things you observe from the corners of your eyes in person, things that would have been out of view on a video screen.

Geography also introduces time zone challenges for scheduling meetings when many people must be coordinated. It also introduces a factor of engagement, since the meeting may occur at the end of a very long day for some of the team. I will be the first to admit that I wasn't as active a participant as I should have been in conference meetings when I had to get up at 4:00 a.m. or start the call at midnight.

Your recipe for the laws would certainly put more emphasis on having things written and ensuring that you are communicating rather than disseminating information. For the laws that depend on physical presence (like MBWA), you need to get creative and maximize opportunities when they come up. In my case with the people that worked for me in Pune, India (yes, this was a real scenario), I would fly to India every nine months to have physical meetings and updates with the teams in the different locations. During that time, I would schedule times throughout the visit to go around to all the teams and say hello, thank them for their contributions, and generally engage in small talk. It was a great way of getting to know people and sometimes to catch up with others.

Here is a tip for managing teams from Asia and South America. Don't be afraid to talk about your family and show interest in theirs. Those cultures really do believe in "family first," and they show immense pride in their achievements. My teams loved to feel connected like family, and, if you achieve that, you will be rewarded with true loyalty.

One other activity I would do to enhance my MBWA practice in Pune was to attend their monthly social. I learned after my first trip that the team picked one day per month to bring the group together in the evening to have some fun and celebrate the birthdays of that month. By coincidence, one of my first trips to Pune coincided with their monthly social, and they very graciously invited me and the North American team to join in the festivities. It was such a great experience that I asked the Pune team leaders to coordinate that event with my future visits so I could participate. This was a powerful time to get to know what was going on in the office and in people's lives.

Age

This has become a very important topic for managers. The generational difference in work styles and motivations have never been as great as they are now. In the current workforce you can have a mix of people who grew up in an age where you worked for a company for life and millennials and members of Gen Z, where there is much more emphasis on lifestyle and social awareness. The younger people will choose to work for organizations based on those criteria and are not afraid to transition to other organizations if the companies' values don't align with theirs.

The recipe for the laws does need to be adjusted based on the generation(s) you are managing.

Motivation

It is important to recognize that people have different motivations when it involves their work. Some are purely motivated by financial compensation. A good friend of mine whom I worked with for years used to openly tell everyone that he was coin-operated. It is somewhat a simplistic view of his motivation, but it sure helps others to understand where he is coming from. Others seek recognition and acknowledgement of their work.

When using Moore's Laws to motivate people, make sure you emphasise the areas that matter to them.

Change

Change is a major factor in managing an organization, and the type of change will dictate how you manage people and the organization. I have found that people like consistency and predictability and that change usually pushes people out of their comfort zone. This may seem like a contradiction, since we often hear that people are bored and want excitement, adventure, and challenges. I believe that most people prefer that exciting changes occur in the peripheral areas of their home and work lives rather than in the main, essential areas.

Core values and beliefs, the ones that drive your life and shape who you are, is a different story. Changes in those areas are quite scary for individuals, because they pose uncertainty and a high potential of failure. People closer to the end of their career embrace change even less than those at the start.

I have often found it ironic that one of the departments most resistant to work change is information technology—ironic because much of its role is implementing systems and services that change *other* people's work lives. I guess we can see an analogy with the idea that doctors make the worst patients.

If you are responsible for developing and implementing change in your organization, a big factor to consider is, "What is the rate of change people, and this organization, can handle?" Some organizations are very agile and thrive in a dynamic environment, but others are institutions that require consistency to maximize predictability of delivery and people's understanding of the process. Size comes into play as well; a small company can implement change much faster than a large one, simply due to the logistics of training the workforce.

The priorities for management during change are:

1. Management must be much more engaged in the human factors and transition anxieties. Be prepared to spend a lot more time listening and repeating the same messages many times to gain acceptance.

2. Deal firmly with people who do not conform or refuse to change.

3. Continually cite the successful progress of the change and demonstrate, with examples, how it is benefiting specific areas.

It is true that not all will benefit to the same degree in an organization, so when that occurs it's worth discussing the broader benefits. Show that other areas are getting significant benefits and for the organization as a whole it is the right direction to move.

So, as the title of this chapter implies, it is not just the ingredients of Moore's Laws that will make you a successful manager, but the way you as a leader combine the ingredients, how you emphasise them, and how you adjust the delivery based on the feedback you get.

Future Disruptors of Management

In the year 2040, the landscape of management underwent a seismic shift, propelled by the relentless march of technological advancement. Gone were the days of corner offices and water cooler chats; instead, the virtual workplace had become the new norm. Artificial intelligence, once a mere tool, had evolved into a sentient collaborator, reshaping the very fabric of how businesses operated.

In the heart of Silicon Valley amid the gleaming skyscrapers and bustling streets stood Innovatech, Inc., a pioneer in AI-driven solutions. At its helm was Dr. Emily Chen, a visionary leader who had anticipated the transformative power of technology on the workforce.

As Dr. Chen strode through the halls of Innovatech, she couldn't help marveling at the bustling energy of her virtual workplace. Teams from across the globe seamlessly collaborated in virtual meeting rooms, their avatars exchanging ideas in real time. Gone were the constraints of geography; talent was sourced from every corner of the globe, each member bringing a unique perspective to the table.

Yet, for all its benefits, the virtual workplace presented its own set of challenges. The lack of face-to-face interaction threatened to erode camaraderie, while the constant barrage of notifications often left employees feeling overwhelmed. Dr. Chen knew that to thrive in this new era, traditional management practices would have to adapt.

Enter Mia, Innovatech's AI-powered management assistant. Programmed with advanced natural language processing capabilities, Mia acted as a digital concierge, guiding employees through their daily tasks and offering personalized recommendations for professional development. From scheduling meetings to providing real-time feedback, Mia streamlined workflows and fostered a culture of continuous improvement.

But Mia was more than just a digital assistant; she was a mentor, a confidante, and a friend. Through sophisticated sentiment analysis algorithms, Mia could detect signs of burnout or disengagement, proactively reaching out to offer support and resources. In a world where mental health had become an increasingly pressing issue, Mia's empathetic presence provided a much-needed lifeline for employees struggling to cope with the demands of the virtual workplace.

Of course, the integration of AI into the workforce was not without its skeptics. Some feared that machines would replace human workers altogether, relegating them to the sidelines of progress. But Dr. Chen saw things differently. To her, AI was not a threat, but a catalyst for innovation. By automating mundane tasks and augmenting human capabilities, AI empowered employees to focus on what truly mattered: creativity, collaboration, and critical thinking.

As the years passed, Innovatech continued to thrive, its workforce propelled by the symbiotic relationship between humans and machines. Dr. Chen's vision had become a reality, ushering in a new era of management focused on harnessing the collective potential of the virtual workplace and AI.

In the annals of corporate history, Dr. Emily Chen would be remembered not only as a pioneer in technological innovation but as a trailblazer in the evolution of management itself. For in the face of unprecedented disruption, she dared to envision a future where humans and machines worked together in harmony, forever changing the way we define success in the modern era.

Managing the New Workforce

Managing the new workforce, characterized by virtual workplaces and AI integration, comes with its own challenges:

1. **Communication and collaboration.** In a virtual environment, effective communication can be hindered by technological barriers and lack of face-to-face interaction. Managers must find ways to foster collaboration and maintain team cohesion across geographical boundaries.

2. **Employee engagement.** Without the physical presence of coworkers, employees may feel isolated and disconnected from the company culture. Managers need to devise strategies to keep remote workers engaged and motivated, ensuring they feel valued and connected to the organization's mission.

3. **Work-life balance.** The boundary between work and personal life can become blurred in a virtual workplace, leading to burnout and decreased productivity. Managers must promote work-life balance by setting clear expectations, encouraging time management practices, and respecting employees' boundaries.

4. **Skill development and training.** With rapid technological advances, employees need to continuously update their skills to remain relevant in the workforce. Managers must prioritize training and development initiatives to upskill employees and ensure they can adapt to evolving job roles and responsibilities.

5. **Performance evaluation:** Traditional methods of performance evaluation may not be suitable for remote or AI-driven work environments. Managers need to implement new metrics and assessment tools to accurately evaluate employee performance and provide constructive feedback.

6. **Data security and privacy.** Since virtual workplaces rely heavily on technology, ensuring data security and protecting employee privacy become paramount. Managers must implement robust cybersecurity measures and adhere to strict privacy regulations to safeguard sensitive information.

7. **Managing diversity and inclusion.** Virtual workplaces can pose challenges in fostering diversity and inclusion, as cultural differences may be amplified in a global workforce. Managers must promote diversity awareness, create inclusive policies, and foster a culture of respect and acceptance.

8. **Adapting to AI integration.** Integrating AI into the workforce requires careful planning and management. Managers must address concerns about job displacement, retrain employees to work alongside AI systems, and ensure that AI technologies are used ethically and responsibly.

Successfully managing the new workforce requires adaptability, empathy, and forward-thinking leadership. By addressing these challenges head-on and embracing technological advancements, managers can create thriving virtual workplaces where employees feel empowered, supported, and motivated to achieve their full potential.

So, Does Management Need to Embrace AI?

Absolutely, management needs to embrace AI to stay competitive and effectively navigate the challenges of the future workforce. Here's why:

1. **Data-driven decision-making.** AI can analyse vast amounts of data in real-time, providing valuable insights that can inform strategic decision-making. By leveraging AI-powered analytics, managers can make more informed and data-driven decisions, leading to better outcomes for the organization.

2. **Efficiency and automation.** AI technologies can automate repetitive tasks, freeing up managers to focus on more strategic and value-added activities. From scheduling meetings to processing invoices, AI-powered automation can streamline workflows and increase operational efficiency.

3. **Personalized employee development.** AI-driven tools can analyse employee performance data and provide personalized recommendations for skill development and career advancement. By leveraging AI in talent management processes, managers can support the professional growth of their team members and enhance overall workforce productivity.

4. **Predictive insights.** AI algorithms can analyse patterns and trends to make predictive forecasts about future events, such as market trends or employee turnover. By harnessing the power of predictive analytics, managers can anticipate potential challenges and proactively address them before they escalate.

5. **Enhanced customer experience.** AI-powered chatbots and virtual assistants can provide round-the-clock customer support, enhancing the overall customer experience. By integrating AI

into customer relationship management processes, managers can improve customer satisfaction and loyalty.

6. **Risk management.** AI can help identify and mitigate risks by analyzing data for potential threats or anomalies. Whether it's detecting fraudulent activities or identifying cybersecurity vulnerabilities, AI-powered risk management tools can help managers protect the organization from potential harm.

7. **Innovation and creativity.** AI technologies can facilitate creativity and innovation by providing new tools and capabilities for problem-solving and idea generation. From generative design to predictive modeling, AI can inspire and augment human creativity, leading to breakthrough innovations.

So, embracing AI is essential for management to leverage the full potential of technology and drive organizational success in the future. By embracing AI-powered tools and methodologies, managers can enhance decision-making, improve operational efficiency, and foster a culture of innovation and continuous improvement.

In summary, you as a manager must be cognizant of the major disruptors in management over the next decade. I believe the big three are:

1. *The workforce of the 2020s.* Clearly, workers entering the workforce in the 2020s have different priorities and values from workers of the previous decade, and their motivation is entirely different from the workforce of the previous century. Learning what is important to them and using that for motivation along with the new work environment, and AI will be critical.

2. *Virtual working.* COVID-19 accelerated working from home and sourcing skilled labor has ushered in the virtual workgroups where resources can be pooled from all over the world. The efficiencies have been proven, but the challenges of maintaining

human interaction and personalization must be addressed to keep people from feeling isolated.

3. *New methods.* AI is a step change for management, and the world will continue to find new and imaginative ways to use the technology. Management is only one aspect of the world's use for it.

As proof of the necessity of dealing with future disruptors, this chapter of the book, up to this summary, was written in collaboration with ChatGPT. Yes, I had to give it the framework and had to go through a few iterations to fine-tune the main points, so this technology must be given good direction for it to produce high-quality results, at least as of the time of writing, in late 2024. The results, though, are impressive, and my personal experience was that AI saved me about 20 to 25 percent of the time I would have spent writing this chapter.

So, Who Is a Good Manager?

Now we are coming full circle to the beginning of the book, where, when I discussed people's careers and opportunities with them, many said they wanted to be managers, and my favourite response was "Why?"

Their biggest reasons were usually the financial benefits, the ability to shape the direction of the work, their sense of being in control, and their sense that being managers was what they needed to feel successful. Most of these reasons are about them, which is perfectly natural. But let's look at these reasons to see how true they are.

I will receive more financial benefit. This is marginally true but, in this day and age, more acknowledgement is being given to individual contributors with a specialized skill, and they are being aligned with first- and even second-level management pay bands. So, if you have a passion for a technical role, stick with it. Also, if financial gain is your primary driver, then sales is a far more lucrative role that, in many situations, will pay more than management. The challenge in sales is the risk factor; sure, if you do well you will be very well compensated, but if you do not perform, you can easily find yourself out the door. Risk, which is directly linked to compensation, is factored by:

- size and age of the company;
- whether you are generating new business or business only with established clients;
- the complexity of the product you are selling; and
- whether your product is a commodity or specialized.

The ultimate path to financial reward is going the entrepreneurial path and starting your own business, in which case you get the management and risk all in one!

I am able to shape the direction of the work. Yes, managers do have influence in shaping the direction of the work; the higher you go in an organization, the greater your strategic influence. But most managers are generally more responsible for how direction is going to be executed, not what the direction is going to be. This area of the manager's job has been very rewarding to me, but also very challenging, as sometimes you are not fully on board with a strategic direction.

As an example in my career, I was brought into the negotiation of outsourcing our IT organization. Senior management had been advised it was a significant cost saving. I personally was not a believer, since it was hard to imagine that an organization with virtually the same number of resources to execute the work required could do it more cost effectively than we could, given that an outsource organization still needs to make a profit. Still, as a manager, I had to negotiate, plan, and execute a transition that generated savings.

In the end, after several years, there were benefits, and outsourcing was the right thing for the organization to do after all. The difficult part of that work wasn't the strategy. It was being on the management team that laid off two-thirds of our organization in one day. What made it even more challenging was that the people didn't even know it was coming, since all our discussions were kept highly confidential. It had to be one of the most stressful and difficult days of my life, and I had moments in that process where I literally said to myself, "I don't get paid enough for this shit." The bottom line for your ability to set direction is that things are rarely within your complete control, and sometimes you can feel like you are just executing instructions. Another thing to remember is that you will have heartbreaking times, and you just have to hang in there. It will get better.

I am in control. This is a great one, because who is really ever in control? We live in a dynamic world where we must expect the unexpected to happen. A manager must be able to roll with the changes, make them happen as smoothly as possible, and minimize disruption. The other reality of control is that everyone has someone they report to. Even the CEO must report to a board of directors, and they in turn are held accountable by the shareholders. You see more and more shareholder activists that move in to take control of an organization if they feel it is being mismanaged. Rick George, an inspiring and great CEO of Suncor, once made a profound statement that really stuck with me.

He said that we, the Suncor Company, had been given the privilege of operating and managing one of the greatest natural resource assets in the world. The world will always need this resource, and if we don't do a good job of managing that asset, the world would find someone else to do it.

Rick really understood that even the head of an organization is not in complete control and is dispensable, particularly if they weren't doing a good job.

This is what I need to feel successful. I believe this reason comes mainly from societal pressures. We have put a lot of emphasis in our Western culture that you can only be successful if we rise to a level of authority in our career. The more you control, the more successful you are. While I can't disagree with this perspective completely, many people use this as the only relevant metric of success and as a result strive for roles that they are not well suited to. When a person goes down this road, they will eventually fall victim to the Peter Principle, the idea that a person will rise only to their level of incompetence. The place you eventually reach is anything but satisfying, not to mention very stressful, too. A person's success should come from being able to do a job well at any level. It is good to push your abilities and try to expand your roles, but there is a critical time that one has to be introspective and admit that this is the best I can do and to be happy with it.

To me, if you want to be a manager, it's all about the people. Therefore you must want to be a good:

Teacher/Mentor

A manager is a teacher and mentor first and foremost. Your role is to apply your wisdom and experience and help those in your group learn from you, particularly when you discuss your failures. You want your people not to make the same mistakes you did. If you aren't feeling a sense of pride when a student of yours is successful, then you shouldn't be a manager.

A teacher needs to be sure the student has understood the lesson or concept correctly. If not, you must find another way to teach that lesson and be patient when you or that person becomes frustrated.

As a mentor, you are there to give a person a different perspective on what they are doing or want to do. Mentoring is more of a long-term perspective for people. It is too easy to be caught up in the day-to-day hustle of life and miss key moments where you must act on opportunities that have long-term benefits. A mentor is one who helps you with this.

Coach

Good management is not just about having several individual contributors, it's about how the team functions as a cohesive unit. The function of the coach is to make a group of individuals function as one unit, to have the group be greater than the sum of its parts. A coach works with members of the team to show how they can interact with each other, build trust and confidence, and ensure that they have each other's backs.

When you coach the team, give them a goal to strive for. A good coach can read the other team's strengths and weaknesses and prepare their own team to get the job done. All these sports analogies do map onto the work environment. You are imparting the overall goal for the team, you are giving the team a heads-up on what to expect when doing a job, and you are ensuring you have coverage and backup in the workplace so that no one person is critical.

Motivator

Work can be tedious and repetitious. Every person can lose interest and focus. You as a manager are responsible for keeping up a team's motivation. Every person needs that individual who is your fan; the person who makes you feel good about what you do and reminds you of what you are working towards is a good thing. Being a motivator is positive for the company and for the motivator.

Visionary

If you just tell people what to do and what the next steps are, you are missing out on the full potential of your team. When you give your team a vision, where you are trying to go and why that's a good thing, you increase engagement.

Vision enables people to be more motivated and can look at the breakdown of work to enable it with a lens of understanding how they contribute to the big picture. The benefit you obtain from a workforce that understands the vision is that they will use their expertise to suggest improvements to the tasks assigned to them, not just execute them and blame the instructions if things don't go well.

When inputs and outputs are better understood, a workforce will require less oversight and usually will come up with efficiencies you never thought of. Someone who has been given a vision is a much more powerful force, because they understand the endpoint and can give you a different perspective to get there.

I have only scratched the surface of the roles of teacher/mentor, coach, motivator, and visionary and why I think they are the true reasons you should want to be a manager. If you want to understand these roles further, many online books and materials speak to them. TED Talks are another resource I have also found very useful. These short presentations are usually excellent at getting to the key concepts, and many of them deal with these roles.

It is my belief that you can learn to be a good manager and that in turn makes you a leader. Leadership, though, is not something you learn, but rather is an ability that is gifted to the very few. A great leader doesn't have to work late nights to write inspirational messages, they can inspire as naturally as you and I breathe. A great leader generates loyalty with their actions, not their commands, and a leader is reflective and observant.

The highest priority for a leader is they care more about the people than themselves. I think the best leaders truly believe that when they draw an organization chart, they illustrate it as an upside-down pyramid to demonstrate that the front-line people are on top—the most important people of the organization. Management enables the people on the front line to perform their best.

Final Thoughts for Your Journey

As I discussed early in the book, for parents, we have all thought it would be great if each child came with a manual. Every person is unique, and one size does not fit all. Nor does one size fit all in management, and in its delivery to a team. We all have different character traits and styles that make us unique. You will always have a team with differing experiences, cultures, and biases. These laws will help you get everyone on the same page and allow you to leverage people's skills and abilities.

So, let's do a recap of the laws in the style of David Letterman's Top 10 lists:

Number 10:	Family first
Number 9:	Work to live, don't live to work
Number 8:	WBWA (Management by wandering around)
Number 7:	ACE (Argue, consent, execute)
Number 6:	Be consistent
Number 5:	Communicate, don't disseminate
Number 4:	Shit happens, get over it
Number 3:	It's just a game; don't take it personally
Number 2:	They lie
Number 1:	If it isn't written, it isn't real

Even though you will deliver these laws differently from how I would, the concept and fundamentals of what they stand for will help you to be a good manager. When I had a good manager, they used at least 60 percent of these laws to lead their own teams. So, the good news is that you should have success even while incorporating only some of these laws into practice.

I hope that I have given you as a hitchhiker a lift along your journey. It's time for you to get out of my car and continue your journey to the next level. Undoubtedly, as the disruption chapter discusses, new challenges will arise, and Moore's 10 Laws will need to be revisited. Some may need to be updated, some may need to be deleted, and new ones may be added. Doing so will be your responsibility, and it is my hope that you can take these laws, make them your own, and pass them on to up-and-coming managers. We will always need managers in this society. Having good ones just makes things easier and a lot more fun and fulfilling!

Good luck. I hope your journey is as good as mine has been. Onward, ho!

My good friend Scott Walsh (retired CIO of Pembina Pipeline Corporation and Enerplus, at left) and me enjoying an adventure in the Rocky Mountains in Fairmont, British Columbia, in the summer of 2014. Having peers with whom to discuss your challenges and knowing you'll get good advice with no agenda behind it helps you craft successful decisions and plans. Throughout 30 years of friendship and working together, we always had each other's back. I feel honoured that he placed his faith and trust in me to safeguard his life, since flying in mountains, always a challenge, can also be dangerous.